MW01030085

ISBN 0-9715274-1-5

Published by:
Freeport Publishing
607 Washington Avenue
Savannah, Georgia 31405

Cover graphic design by T-Square Graphics
Savannah, Georgia

Printed by Rose Printing Company
Tallahassee, Florida

Preface

It seems so long ago. Most of us today, even those of us living in Savannah, are totally unaware of it. Some know a battle of the Revolutionary War was fought in Savannah but don't know why, who won, or why it is even worthy of mention. Those a little more knowledgeable will say, "you don't hear much about it because the patriots lost." While this is true it still leaves one to wonder why such an important part of our American heritage has been forgotten. Why this battle, where more lives were lost and casualties suffered in one hour than any other encounter of the war, has been brushed aside by history?

Most of the emphasis of the Revolutionary War as taught in our schools is on the northern states and major battles in those campaigns. The names of Lexington & Concord, Bunker Hill and Saratoga all have a familiar ring and engender a patriotic fervor to our ears. Many are unaware of the southern campaigns and their importance, not only to the overall strategy of the war leading to Yorktown, but of the brutality brought by the British in their methods of waging war on the American citizens.

The patriots in Savannah did fail in their attempt to subdue the British but it's important not to overlook the results of what took place. The failure of the assault by French and American forces upon British lines, where Count Pulaski was mortally wounded, affected the entire course of the Revolutionary War. After the battle, British Gov. Wright of Georgia said, "if the province had fallen, the colonies would have been lost to Britain. Gen. Prevost's troops have preserved the Empire."

Ron Freeman

Table of Contents

1.   Colonial Savannah 1

2.   Florida Fiascos 10

3.   The British Attack Savannah.. 19

4.   Lincoln Takes Command. . . .. .27

5.   Kettle Creek. 34

6.   Briar Creek. 40

7.   Charleston and Stono Ferry. 48

8.   France to the Rescue. .54

9.   British Reaction 57

10.   The Patriots March. 65

11.   D'Estaing's Demand. 70

12.   The British Fortify 74

13.   Maitland's Determination. 79

14.   Allies Dig In.. 86

15.   Savannah Under Siege 92

16.   The Forlorn Hope 101

17.   October 9th. 114

18. Glory at a Price. 125

19. Retreat. 132

20. Aftermath. 135

21. Allied Withdrawal. .139

22. Assessment. 144

23. Epilogue 147

24. Illustrations. 158

25. References. 163

26. Illustration Credits .167

27. Index 168

Savannah under Siege

Colonial Savannah

At the outbreak of the Revolutionary War in 1775, the town of Savannah and the colony of Georgia only has forty-two years of history. Remember that Georgia is the last of the original thirteen colonies to be chartered. It was founded in 1733 by a group of English trustees and for almost twenty years was under their guidance and protection. Only in the twenty years before the American Revolution has it become a royal colony under the governance of a succession of three royal governors. Georgia's population is small, only about 40,000 with half of those being slaves. There are barely 3,000 men of military age.

Being so unpopulated, Georgia is almost helpless in defending itself. Because of this Congress passes special legislation to allow the state to recruit in other states in an effort to fill its militia ranks and even passes a special subsidy of $1 million dollars to aid the state in its efforts for defense. Most of the people are located in a fifty-mile strip south of the Savannah River. The major areas of density other than Savannah are Sunbury, about thirty miles down the coast from Savannah and Augusta, about 110 miles upriver. In addition to its other problems, Georgia's currency is so inflated that those outside the state will not even accept it.

Georgians, in step with the other American colonies, protest what they feel to be excessive taxation from England but are not as eager as their northern neighbors to join in the revolutionary movement. Many of the causes of discontent in the other twelve colonies are not present in Georgia. With its thriving plantation system, it fits well into the British mercantile plan. Also, many of the colony's citizens, unlike those to the north, are native-born Englishmen.

Georgia has become the pet of Parliament owing largely to the fact that it has provided more than a million pounds for the colony's support. In Savannah, most residents are British first, then Georgians, and lastly Americans. In Georgia as a colony, the population is even more divided. The wealthier merchant-planter class wants to keep its ties with England, whereas the less prosperous citizens want independence. This group includes not only tradesmen and artisans in its ranks, but surprisingly some of the sons of prominent loyalists.

When the tariff controversy began, there were many first generation Englishmen still alive in Georgia. Most fathers retained their loyalty to England while their sons clamored for freedom. The rebels established a patriot government and claimed it to be the legal governing body of the colony. Archibald Bulloch, an ancestor of President Theodore Roosevelt, became its first president and after his unexpected death, Button Gwinnett, one of the signers of the Declaration of Independence, succeeded him as the second.

The British royal governor, James Wright, has been rendered powerless. He attempts to reconvene the royal assembly, but it is in vain. The members refuse. Governor Wright is then arrested by young Joseph Habersham of the patriots and confined to house arrest. Wright gives his word he will not attempt to escape. In spite of this, he slips away and leaves the colonies on the British man-of-war, *Scarborough.*

After the Articles of Confederation, America's first blueprint for government, are enacted in 1777, the city braces itself for war with the British. At the outset of the war, most of the active struggle and significant battles are taking place in the major northern cities but word is then received there is a coming change in strategy. British eyes are turning southward.

Why, and why Savannah? Why of the entire south is it so important to England? Apparently, for two reasons. First, the southern states are thinly populated but with vocal British sentiment and because of this, possess an inherent military weakness. Secondly, there is a popular conception among the British that there is a good deal of latent Tory sentiment in these backwoods states.

These reasons draw the thoughts of King George like a magnet to the possibility of back door warfare against Gen. George Washington's army in the North. At the end of 1778, after three years of war, the two sides have reached something of a stalemate. Now, if the British can only subdue Georgia, it will greatly facilitate their overland invasion into South Carolina and then into the upper regions of the South.

By 1778, George Washington has regained Philadelphia and many other sites. The king is continuing to tell his generals how to run the war in America even though he is 3,000 miles away. When the British lose the battle at Saratoga in New York, King Louis XVI of France, prodded by Benjamin Franklin and the Marquis de Lafayette, enters a treaty to help America.

The patriot's victory is the show of strength needed to convince France that America would pursue the war to final success. The two countries sign two treaties. The first, a treaty of amity and commerce, officially recognizes the new country and encourages Franco-American trade. The second provides for a military alliance against Great Britain and recognition of the United States as a condition of peace.

Now, transport yourself back in time to Savannah in 1778. What does it look like and what do you observe? If you stand on the bluff overlooking the river, in every direction there are rice fields and savannas stretching as far as the eye can see. Savannah is still a modest seaport town cut out of a small clearing in the piney woods.

Savannah, to outsiders, is probably thought of more in terms of the river and port rather than the town. When people refer to Savannah they don't mean just the town but the surrounding plantations that are connected by crude but passable roads. Beyond the town the road system is limited by having only three main arteries.

To the north, leading to Zubley's ferry on the Savannah River and South Carolina beyond is the Augusta (Louisville) Road. To the south, connecting with Midway and ultimately Darien is the Ogeechee Road that becomes an extension of Bull Street about a half-mile from the river. It was laid out over old Indian trails under the guidance of Tomochichi, a chief and early friend to the colony and Gen. Oglethorpe, its founder. Finally, there is the Sea Island Road, forking out toward the small settlements of Thunderbolt and Beaulieu (Bew-lee) and then all the rivers and creeks along the seaboard of Georgia and the Carolinas.

Savannah is a small town whose population is still insignificant although it has become swollen with the war. The normal population is only about seven hundred and fifty residents living and working in four hundred and fifty frame buildings. The streets are yet unpaved.

The soil is extremely sandy, which not only makes walking difficult but also results in the houses being filled with dust during the dry and windy summer season. From east to west the town is about a half mile in distance. It is a little over a quarter mile from north to south. South Broad (Oglethorpe Avenue) has only a few houses and these are on the north side of the street. There are only two residential suburbs. On the east is Trustees' Garden, a ten-acre tract initially dedicated to determining what types of plants could best be cultivated in Georgia. On the west is the Yamacraw Settlement composed of a cluster of

Savannah Under Siege

houses and gardens.

Houses in Savannah are basically of two types. Some are small and poorly constructed and these contrast with large solid homes crowded along the business district. Most of the shops have painted signs but instead of giving the proprietor's name, the sign is usually an emblem such as that found over the door of a tavern or inn.

In many cases businesses and dwelling houses are under the same roof. The buildings are two stories with the shop occupying the front of the first story and the rest of the structure used as living quarters. Ashes and garbage are thrown without regard into alleys or dumped on vacant lots. Stray horses, cows, hogs and even goats roam the streets consuming the refuse.

Savannah is bordered on the north by the river and surrounded on three other sides by swampy marshlands containing luxuriant rice fields and endless pine forests.

There are no notable buildings in town other than the Episcopal Church on Bull Street about which the architecture is not significant. Additional buildings are the governor's mansion, the market, the old silk house, or Filature, and of course the public taverns where the wines and ales are in abundance and the food is served with good taste. The social and political life of the colonial capital of Georgia revolves around the governor's house on St. James (Telfair) Square.

Many planters left the state at the beginning of the war and now keenly watch from safety outside its borders to determine the outcome before taking sides. The Americans order these people to return and cultivate the land they claim or within six months they will forfeit title and it will be given to another. In 1776, with the arrest of the Royal Governor, the Americans confiscated the estates of most loyalists in Savannah. In these revolutionary times, Savannah is a city of trade and commerce without the smoke and grime of factories. There are no screaming whistles and no roaring traffic; only the sound of the carpenter's hammer and saw and the voices of the citizens as they go about their daily business. Savannah's port before the war flourished with export trade in rice, lumber, pitch, hides and indigo.

So why is the town so important to the British as a military objective? Because the British feel Savannah is their steppingstone for invading Carolina. From there they can salvage the southern colonies for the Crown. Savannah is also the only port south of Charleston with facilities to receive and service a sloop of war.

George III of England analyzes in detail every military and naval action in the colonies. He even suggests strategy and formulates the plans for implementation. These plans now call for an offensive against the southern colonies with an immediate plan to conquer Georgia and South Carolina. He feels that once South Carolina has been re-established as a royal colony, it will be a simple task to hike northward to the area of the Chesapeake. North Carolina is considered to be no more than a path leading to Virginia.

The newly appointed commander of the southern forces for the patriots is Gen. Benjamin Lincoln. For over a year the rotund Lincoln has been inactive, suffering from a severe leg wound he received at Saratoga. Because of this, he is affected with a conspicuous limp. He writes to Washington that he is apprehensive about making the long journey from New England to the south with the condition of his leg. However, Lincoln is a soldier. He knows where his ultimate duty lies and because of this, he begins traveling south.

Soon after reaching Charleston, the new commander learns the British are moving against Georgia by both land and sea. Gen. Augustine Prevost (Pray-vo) is moving up from Florida and a British deserter has divulged the coming of a British fleet from New York with several thousand troops destined for Savannah.

After accepting the appointment, Lincoln's first priority is to raise an army but he has no money allotted for the task. He will have to appeal to the four state governors within his department for financial assistance. In order to meet the threat of the anticipated British invasion, the new leader in the southern theater must meet the challenge of assembling an army. He must recruit a number of regulars, who are referred to as continentals, as well as extend the enlistment period for a majority of the militia, which is always questionable.

The militia is the name for the reserve army that is under the control of each state's governor. They are usually poorly trained and part-time soldiers at best. They normally can't be counted on because in most cases, the moment a militiaman's brief term of service has expired, he shoulders his rifle and heads for home. Lincoln also discovers that even with the few soldiers he has returning, only a small number of these are physically fit for duty.

At the break from England, America was not a united country but thirteen independent states. The only governing body was the Continental Congress but it was toothless since it possessed no power to raise a military or to levy taxes. It could only recommend a budget for funding the military and ask each state to meet its quota in proportion to its wealth and population.

To further confuse matters, each state had its own militia, or army, and it competed with the continental recruiters in obtaining men. The states also could offer their inductees financial inducements and a shorter period of enlistment, one year at most, compared to three years or the duration of the war for the continentals. If one were reasonably intelligent and from a middle-class background, a commission in either the continental line or the militia was often obtainable.

There was resentment too on the part of state militias that regarded officers in the continental army as outsiders. Even the governors regarded them as interlopers since only Congress had a voice in their selection. This meant as a continental officer, you needed to be a diplomat and politician to cajole cooperation from the various states and their militias.

Since all the King's efforts in the North have failed to crush the rebellion, he decides to make another attempt against a lightly defended South. If Georgia and the Carolinas can be subdued, then the surrender of the North should follow close behind. Agreeing with the King's logic, Gen. Clinton, as British commander-in-chief, orders a special squadron to be assembled in New York. It totals about thirty-five hundred men under the command of Col. Archibald Campbell and embarks from Sandy Hook, New Jersey on November 27, 1778. His force consists of the 71st Regiment of Highlanders, two battalions of Hessians, four battalions of loyalists and a detachment of royal artillery under the escort of a squadron of royal navy commanded by Commodore Hyde Parker.

The Hessians are German troops hired by King George III to aid in suppressing the American colonies. They were the answer to Britain's shortage of troops due to the majority of their forces being stationed in other areas of their far-flung empire. For almost a century German rulers had used their armies as a lucrative source of revenue. Their availability was one of the primary reasons England and other nations could maintain small standing armies in peacetime. Negotiations had taken place between the King's emissaries and German princes to supply a substantial number of well-trained troops to serve in America. Close to thirty thousand German soldiers are allied with the British in America. Approximately seventy-five hundred of these soldiers and officers will lose their life in battle or through sickness and accidents, and about another six thousand men, will remain in Canada and Nova Scotia when the war ends.

The basic military unit in the British army was the regiment. Each consisted of eight companies and two flank companies. The flank companies were usually light infantries that were quick moving and skilled marksmen. They were often assigned to scouting, reconnaissance, and other special duties. They were considered the best soldiers in the regiment. A regiment at full strength consisted of 410 men and officers.

Recruits were trained in loading and firing until they could discharge three rounds per minute. This was done on command since firing was to be done in volleys as called for by the tactical doctrine of the day. Twelve separate orders were required between each fire.

Volleys were usually exchanged at about 40 yards and it was always possible that flying ramrods were part of the exchange as well as bullets. The standard method of attacking was to advance within 40 yards, discharge your weapon and then charge with the bayonet. It was extremely effective, especially against new troops.

Mounted troops were either cavalry or dragoons. The distinction was that cavalry fought on horseback whereas dragoons were simply mounted infantries who rode to battle but fought on foot. However in the southern campaigns, all mounted troops were referred to as dragoons and performed the tasks of scouting, mounted charges upon the enemy, pursuing a retreating enemy and fighting from horseback. In both armies the cavalry provided the eyes for the commanding officers.

Col. Campbell is a Member of Parliament representing the Stirling boroughs of Scotland and the son of the Commissioner of the Western Isles. He is a Scotsman through and through. He was taken prisoner after landing in patriot-controlled Boston but after two years exchanged for Ethan Allen of Green Mountain Boys fame.

H. Ronald Freeman

Florida Fiascos

The southern invasion calls for Col. Campbell to ultimately join forces with Gen. Augustine Prevost, British commander in East Florida. Prevost has been waiting for some time for the opportunity to move northward on a Georgia invasion. In appearance, he could be mistaken for George Washington except for a circular scar near his temple. Prevost is a veteran of many years service in the British army. Actually, Prevost is not even British by birth but a Swiss soldier of fortune. The Swiss-born officer is wounded at Fontenoy in 1745. During the battle of Quebec with the French in 1759, he receives an additional wound that leaves a circular depression on his temple and leads to his being nicknamed "Old Bullet Head."

East Florida is how the peninsular is referred to, as opposed to West Florida, which is called the panhandle. Prevost's troops are garrisoned at St. Augustine, the capital. The town was founded by the Spaniards many years before and has become a haven for British loyalists from Georgia. Early on, from the outbreak of the war, Prevost had petitioned British Gen. Howe, and his successor Gen. Clinton, for reinforcements that will allow him to mount an invasion of Georgia to the north. This means, for the patriots in Georgia, that Florida is an ever-present threat.

There have been repeated raids from the Florida Tories into south Georgia, primarily for purposes of stealing the patriots' cattle. Finally the Georgia patriots have had enough and in April 1777, they decide to mount a campaign against St. Augustine to stamp out that bed of Toryism. It is of good intent but it has a major problem in execution. Its trouble is that there are two factions in the Georgia army and they are at odds with each other.

Button Gwinnett leads the state militia. As of March 1777, he is the newly appointed president of Georgia and one of the recent signers of the Declaration of Independence. The continental army is headed by Gen. Lachlan McIntosh, a Scotsman with vast military experience. McIntosh receives a promotion to brigadier general when he assumes the command. His commission is earlier than Gwinnett's appointment and bears the date of September 1776.

Gwinnett's ego gets in the way and he is furious when McIntosh is chosen over him to lead the continental forces into Florida. He even has McIntosh's younger brother George, arrested for treason on the charge that he is part of a scheme to sell rice to enemy Tories in Florida (George McIntosh is later acquitted). When the expedition to Florida is ready to depart, Gwinnett insists that he go along and even appoints Samuel Elbert, who is second in command under McIntosh, as commander of the continental forces rather than McIntosh as is his due.

Gwinnett himself leads the militia, claiming that in his capacity as president of the state he is entitled to the command. He instructs Elbert that he is to receive his orders only from him and his council. Elbert quickly points out the irregularity to the council as well as to Gwinnett. He is ignored. In turn, he asks Gen. McIntosh to give him guidance on what he should do. McIntosh counsels him against mutiny and advises him to obey Gwinnett's orders.

Gwinnett's is more a political mind than military and his idea is that all they have to do is cross the St. Mary's River, separating Georgia from Florida, hoist the liberty flag and make a showing with the army, all the while encouraging the people to change allegiances. Finally due to problems in recruiting, he is forced to request aid from McIntosh and his continental army but only at the final moment and only because so few militia can be raised.

Prevost knows he doesn't stand a ghost of a chance in defending St. Augustine with only a token force unless his command is reinforced from New York. It isn't. But as it turns out, neither is it necessary. The Georgia expedition turns into a comedy. Both continental troops and militia set out for Sunbury, south of Savannah, in early April. Here the old feud between McIntosh and Gwinnett flares again and cooperation proves impossible. The army never even reaches St. Augustine. With two leaders both giving orders, no one knows whose to follow and the army just falls apart. Each insists he commands the expedition and neither will allow the other to issue orders for his troops.

The continental troops under Elbert are positioned at Sunbury and depart for Ft. Frederica about 50 miles south and later to the north end of Amelia Island. There they are scheduled to join up with four hundred troops of the Georgia militia under Col. John Baker. From that point they plan to present a united force to participate in the overrunning of East Florida. As it turns out, Baker is only able to raise a little over a hundred men.

Baker arrives at the St. John's River near St. Augustine before Elbert. While there he is attacked by a combined force of Tories and Indians led by Col. Daniel McGirth. Baker's command is totally dissipated. While most of them make their way back to Georgia settlements, a few do remain in the area and are able to locate and join up with Col. Elbert.

Who is McGirth? Both a deadly shot and superb horseman who initially was an ardent patriot. Noted not only for his bravery but his cruelty, his name strikes terror throughout Georgia. He owns a magnificent horse named Grey Goose that is undoubtedly one of the finest horses in either army. While serving in the American army, a continental officer offered to buy him but McGirth refused. From that point on, the officer made McGirth's life a living hell. Finally exasperated, McGirth struck at the officer but a fellow patriot stayed his hand.

For this indiscretion, McGirth was court martialled and sentenced to ten lashes of cowhide on his bare back.

Savannah Under Siege

Not once but for three days in succession. After the first day at dusk, his back raw, he sat in his jail cell and heard the whinny of Grey Goose. What his captors didn't count on was that McGirth was not only enterprising but possessed great physical strength. He used a broken trowel to loosen the masonry around the window bar and used superhuman strength to pull the bar from its foundation. With barely enough room, he squeezed through the narrow opening and dropped to the ground. With a whistle to Grey Goose, he was gone.

From that moment on, McGirth's mindset was against the Americans and their cause and he sought out the enemy and joined the British army. After changing sides and until the end of the war he became one of the most ferocious fighters against the Americans. His entire nature had been perverted by the harsh treatment he received. In battles he was twice wounded but never taken prisoner even though a huge reward was offered for his capture. The entire countryside was trying to catch him but repeatedly, when they were close, the fleet foot of his best friend, the Grey Goose, saved him. Thus McGirth became a fierce opponent of the poorly led Americans.

The Florida expedition proceeds southward about the same time the British head north from St. Augustine toward the St. Mary's River at the Georgia-Florida border. The British in St. Augustine have been informed of Elbert's approach and send armed schooners and land guns to reinforce existing batteries and intercept him. In addition, British troop reinforcements plus two gunboats are dispatched to the mouth of the St. John's to coordinate with the land forces. This unfavorable shift in circumstances, combined with Baker's defeat, convince Elbert to rethink his mission and retire back to the safety of Frederica.

The Florida expedition was poorly planned and poorly executed. It was conceived because of ambition and jealousy, planned without due caution, marred in execution and utterly without benefit in its results. The time had come for an explanation.

In May of 1777, John Adam Treutlen, a Salzburger of Ebenezer, is elected governor of Georgia. Gwinnett is bitterly disappointed at his defeat and McIntosh does not hesitate to openly avow his gratification at the election of Treutlen. Both Gwinnett and McIntosh are called back to Savannah from Sunbury to explain the reasons for the failure of the Florida campaign to the Committee on Safety, the ruling body of the state at the time. They both appear before the chamber.

Gwinnett is an eloquent speaker and acquits himself well. As a result, the Committee exonerates him of all blame. Next is McIntosh, who is enraged. He calls Gwinnett a scoundrel and a lying rascal right there on the floor of the legislature. This is the final straw and in the days of polite society, it leaves only one course of action for a gentleman so insulted, -- "Pistols at dawn."

The adversaries meet the next morning in a meadow near the eastern outskirts of Savannah. A distance of ten paces is stepped off. On signal, both men fire and both receive shots in the thigh. McIntosh is the more fortunate. His wound is clean whereas Gwinnett has been nicked in the bone. He is taken back to his house where he lies for several days in a fever and during that period, gangrene sets in. On the third day, he dies.

McIntosh is tried and acquitted but still, Gwinnett had powerful friends whose sentiment is strong against him. McIntosh is able to secure a post with Gen. Washington at Valley Forge through the help of his friends, George Walton and Henry Laurens of Charleston. Walton is a signer of the Declaration of Independence from Georgia and has served as his second in the duel. Laurens is from South Carolina and was president of the Second Continental Congress. He is also McIntosh's patron. After McIntosh leaves Georgia, Samuel Elbert is

Savannah Under Siege

promoted to the command of all continental forces in Georgia.

Gen. Prevost, still in St. Augustine, is ordered to march north and unite with Campbell in his attack on Savannah. Opposing them on the American side is forty-seven year old Maj. Gen. Robert Howe of North Carolina. Howe has succeeded Gen. Charles Lee as commander of the Southern Military District. He is from a prominent family and an eloquent and a persuasive speaker. He is popular among men and women are even more attracted to him. Howe has not been very effective in his efforts to bring order out of the chaotic southern military situation.

He has been described as a "ladies man" savoring all that come his way and a man that no woman can resist. He is as equally comfortable with philosophers as with libertines. It is said of Howe by Congress that if the war continues, they hope he will have an opportunity to display his abilities on the field of Mars, as well as he does on the field of Venus. Howe oversees the only American army in the south, about seven hundred continental troops and seven hundred-fifty militia.

Gen. Prevost wants to pull Howe away from Savannah if possible so as not to impede Campbell's expeditionary force in route from New York. As a diversion, he dispatches two forces, one by sea under Col. Lewis V. Fuser (Few-zer) and the other by land under the command of his younger brother, Col. Jean Marcus "Marc" Prevost. Fuser's force, consisting of vessels carrying five hundred British regulars, battering cannons, light artillery and mortars, is to attack Ft. Morris at Sunbury, about twenty miles below Savannah. Prevost's brother, with one hundred regulars, three hundred loyalists, and a number of Creek Indians is to march by land and devastate the lower portion of Georgia before moving to Sunbury and joining up with Fuser.

Col. Prevost enters Georgia unopposed until he

nears Midway, about ten miles west of Sunbury. At that point he runs head on with both continentals and militia. The Americans have set up two pieces of light artillery and constructed breastworks across the road at the head of the causeway over which the British have to advance. They hope to keep Col. Prevost in check until reinforcements can arrive from Savannah.

Gen. James Screven and twenty militiamen join the Americans. Screven has resigned his commission in the continental army and has been commissioned a brigadier general in the Georgia militia. They decide to abandon their location in favor of a more strategic one about a mile and a half south of the Midway Church. At that spot a thick wood skirts the road and it was thought to be a good place to set an ambush.

British Col. McGirth, who is well acquainted with the terrain of south Georgia, and knowing the ground held by the Americans, suggests to Prevost that they place an ambush as well. By chance it is at the very place selected by the Americans. British troops arrive first, a short time before the Americans. As the patriots get there, shots are immediately exchanged. Fierce but sporadic fighting commences.

During a lull in the skirmish, Gen. Screven and Col. Baker advance with a small force and cross a swamp to reconnoiter enemy positions. Baker sees the British first and cries out to Screven, "General, here they are." British troops open fire.

Screven falls from his horse with a severe wound and is set upon immediately by the enemy. As he lies wounded and helpless on the ground, British troops fire their muskets point blank into him. Helpless, he is moved under a flag of truce to the vestry house of the Midway Church. Col. Prevost learns of his condition and dishonorable treatment and dispatches his personal physician to provide care. Screven is given every attention possible but still succumbs as a result of his wounds. He was thirty-four years of age. The Americans, being outnumbered, fall back to the Midway Church as well.

Knowing they are facing greater numbers, a plan of misinformation is devised by the Americans. They forge a communication as though Col. Elbert himself has written it. The letter is dropped at an appropriate place hoping it will fall into enemy hands and be taken to Col. Prevost. It is in fact picked up by British troops and taken to the Colonel. He considers it genuine. The letter orders the Americans to retreat so as to draw the British as far as possible toward Savannah. It states a large body of cavalry has just crossed the Ogeechee River south of Savannah in order to gain the rear of the enemy with plans to capture their entire force.

Although Col. Prevost continues to pursue the retreating Americans, he only advances for about six miles north of Midway. Since Fuser has not yet arrived at Sunbury, Prevost decides to abandon his attack and return to St. Augustine. He turns his troops around and starts marching back to Florida. His is a scorched earth retreat and he blackens his withdrawal with the ruins of settlements, crops and families. In his wake he leaves a burned Midway Church as well as many of the homes and barns within his reach. His force is little more than a horde of freebooters glutting themselves with the blood and spoil of the land.

What Col. Prevost is unaware of is that Col. Fuser has been delayed by strong headwinds and does not arrive at Sunbury until after he has begun his retreat. He is then beyond Fuser's reach of communication. Fuser's armed vessels sail up the Midway River and take positions in front of Ft. Morris and also in the Back River opposite the town. Then his main force, accompanied by field pieces, marches on to Sunbury. Fuser demands of Col. John McIntosh, commander of the fort, that he surrender.

H. Ronald Freeman

McIntosh's garrison consists of only one hundred and twenty-seven continentals, a small number of militia and a few Sunbury citizens. They number less than two hundred in all. McIntosh's laconic reply probably set the tone for many American generals in wars to come. He replies to Fuser if he wants the fort, "come and take it."

Instead of attacking, Fuser hesitates. He awaits a report from his scouts about the precise movements of Prevost and when he might be expected to join him. Of course Prevost has already begun his retreat and is beyond the reach of easy communication.

When Fuser learns that Prevost is heading back to Florida he is both surprised and chagrined and elects to raise the siege. He believes that overcoming the fort is not equal to the risk. Fuser re-embarks his troops and returns to the St. John's River in Florida where he meets the returning forces of Col. Prevost. At that point bitter recriminations ensue between the two officers with each accusing the other of being responsible for the failure of their respective expeditions.

Savannah Under Siege

The British Attack Savannah

After the British retreat, Gen. Howe marches his troops southward to occupy Sunbury. About a quarter of his men are ill having yielded to malaria and other fevers during the east Florida campaigns. Officially Howe has been replaced as commander of southern forces by Gen. Lincoln in September 1778, but still remains in charge of the defenses of Savannah. He only learns of Campbell's intended attack on the 6th of December. Howe also knows from his sources that Gen. Prevost is part of the joint operation and will again be pushing north from Florida to join with Campbell in a combined attack on Savannah.

Howe marches his troops back to Savannah with dispatch and takes a position a half-mile southeast of the town across the main road from the river landings. This places him in a strong position to intercept the British when they come up the river. The town is at his back. A full alert is in effect. The governor orders out the militia and continental forces are summoned from South Carolina. Every effort is made to prepare for the threatened invasion. Howe's force consists of an even mix of continental troops and militia, all-in-all about fifteen hundred men. He is heavily outnumbered.

Campbell's squadron drops anchor off Tybee Island, at the mouth of the Savannah River, on December 23rd, 1778. This puts them about fourteen miles from the town. Since the area between Savannah and the ocean is low and marshy and intercrossed by numerous tidal creeks, the first practical landing place they can find is about twelve miles up the river.

Campbell orders Capt. Sir James Baird to go ashore with a light infantry company on the night of December 25th with orders to reconnoiter the area. Baird captures two American deserters who give him a complete account of the defenses of the city. They reveal that Howe's forces are small, less than half the size of the British army. Campbell knows that as soon as Gen. Lincoln, with a force about equal in size to Howe's, discovers his arrival, he will hasten to join Howe in opposition. Based on the circumstances, Campbell elects to attack without waiting for the arrival of Prevost.

The British fleet includes the man-of-war *Vigilante* the galleys *Comet and Keppel* and the armed sloop *Greenwich.* These are followed by the troop transports with three divisions under Commodore Hyde Parker. They sail upriver and approach Girardeau's plantation about two miles below Savannah. They arrive at this landing about 4:00 in the afternoon of the 28th. At this point a low tide occurs and several of the transports are grounded. The British have to wait until dawn to land.

Early the next morning, the First Battalion of the 71st Regiment and the Loyalist Company of the New York Volunteers are carried in longboats to a levee on the plantation. From that point, a narrow causeway of about eight hundred yards divides flooded rice fields to Brewton Hill, which stands on a bluff. Lt. Col. John Maitland (Mateland) commands the troops.

Samuel Elbert, the commander of Georgia continental troops, had earlier advised Howe to defend this area in force since it is an obvious landing site. It would further strengthen the meager patriot defenses if the rice fields at Brewton Hill are flooded prior to the British landing. Additionally, Howe could place a battery there. Howe will only consent to send a small token body of troops.

John Maitland, commander of the 71st Regiment of Scotch Highlanders is forty-seven years old. Maitland's father is the sixth Earl of Lauderdale in Scotland. At his home in Thirlestane Castle, he had given refuge to Bonnie Prince Charlie after his defeat at Culloden, when John was only a boy. His mother Elizabeth is the daughter of the Earl of Findlater and Seafield, who has served as Lord High

Savannah Under Siege

Chancellor of Scotland.

Maitland, as well as Campbell, has served in the House of Commons but has left his high station and comforts back in Scotland. He is now living the hard life of a soldier in the war torn colonies. His empty right sleeve attests to the fact that he has already fulfilled his duty to King and country. He lost his arm to a cannon ball twenty years earlier in a skirmish in Spain where he was the only commissioned officer wounded.

At the outbreak of the American Revolution he re-entered the Marines with the rank of major. In the fighting in the New England theater he proved himself to be a resourceful and alert officer. Maitland is highly respected by his troops and it is said they will blindly follow him anywhere.

The American officers, as well as the British, respect Maitland. He is personally acquainted with George Washington and after a raid where his men aren't credited, notifies the American commander that his men will begin wearing red feathers in their bonnets. This is so Washington will know it is his Highlanders who should be credited with attacking American posts and convoys. True to his word, until the end of the war, Maitland's regiment wears the red feather.

Howe has dispatched a company of about fifty Americans from the South Carolina continentals to Brewton Hill. There, they fire upon the British as they attempt to land. The Highlanders charge and give them no time to repeat the initial volley. By so doing they drive the Americans into the woods and secure a landing place for the rest of their army.

The road from the landing is flanked on the side near the river with flooded rice fields and on the other by a thickly wooded and seemingly impenetrable swamp. Howe burns the bridge that crosses a small rivulet about a hundred yards in front of the American line. He cuts a parallel trench and with marsh on both sides, it soon fills with water and offers a serious obstacle to the enemy advance. Here Howe places two cannons that flank the causeway and are supported by three others that are aimed directly down the road. Having taken their positions, the Americans await the coming onset.

The left side of the American line near the rice fields, east of today's Ft. Wayne, is made up of Georgia militia under the command of Col. Samuel Elbert. To his right Col. Isaac Huger (You-gee) commands the first South Carolina rifles and Lt. Col. William Thompson's Third Rangers. Even farther right is Col. George Walton, who occupies a few buildings with about a hundred of the Georgia militia.

A cannon supports Walton's troops and combines with two other artillery pieces in the center of the American lines and one on the left flank with Elbert. Howe's headquarters has been established at the Tattnall plantation of Fair Lawn. Today it would be at the intersection of East Broad and Taylor Streets.

The following day, December 29th, the advance guard of British light infantry form their line about eight hundred yards from the American position for the attack on the road. Behind them, another two hundred yards, is the main body, hidden from the Americans by a small rise. Campbell detects from the American deployment that they are expecting an attack on their left. What the Americans do not know is that Campbell, quite by chance, has come upon an old black man named Quamino Dolly, nicknamed "Quash", who offers to guide his troops. For a small "reward", Quash leads the British on a secret path through the wooded swamp that protects the American right.

It is clear that Howe logically thinks the British will have no choice other than to make a direct attack on the American lines. While they outnumber his force almost four-to-one he is confident of the marksmanship of his troops and he has the clear advantage of the high ground.

Savannah Under Siege

Even more, the initial disposition of the British troops seems to bear out his assumption.

Col. Walton, because he has lived in the area and possesses a detailed knowledge of the terrain, warns General Howe of the hidden path. Howe chooses to ignore it. He thinks the chance of the British discovering the path is so remote he need not bother to even defend it. Unaware of the lurking danger, Howe opens with cannon fire on Campbell's line. The enemy makes no response and only waits in silence. Not one of their guns is fired in return.

Everything waits, and while the attention of the patriots is focused on the main British force in front of them, Baird's detachment reaches the White Bluff Road (Bull Street) undetected. From there they rush forward on Walton's flank and rear. Upon hearing the active musket fire to his left, Campbell makes a false attack on his right against the thin American line. He runs his guns forward from their concealed position and opens up on the American position and orders his infantry to charge. His attack is timed on the American front to coincide with that of his main force under Baird that has wended its way through the swamp to the rear of Howe's right.

Suddenly, the Americans are caught between a crossfire and are quickly scattered. Early in the fighting, Walton is felled from his horse, wounded in the hip and taken prisoner, along with a large part of his demoralized brigade that is wounded or captured. Walton will limp for the remainder of his days from the wound.

The Americans, now sandwiched between heavy British forces from two directions, can only flee through Savannah. The only line of retreat is the Augusta Road through Musgrove Swamp, west of the town. This road is bordered on the south by the swamp and on the north by rice fields all the way to the river. British forces charge forward to seize the road and block the American retreat. Fortunately, Howe and some of the American forces reach it ahead of the British. Others are not so lucky.

The right center of the American line under Col. Huger falls back. As they attempt to retreat through the town and through the crossfire, the pursuing British bayonet many of them in the streets. Most of Huger's troops get across the causeway but the left side under Elbert near the river finds the escape sealed and is forced to take to the swamp and rice fields. They throw down their weapons in a desperate attempt to escape. Many are unable to swim and die trying to cross the Musgrove Creek, then at full tide, to reach the Augusta Road. Those lucky enough not to drown, are captured.

As soon as Commodore Parker discovers the British are victorious, he moves his small but armed vessels up to the town. Once there, he secures the shipping and commands the town from all approaches on the Carolina side. This maneuver cuts Savannah totally off from supplies and is accomplished with only one British sailor killed and five wounded. The British victors capture a hundred and twenty-six prisoners and seize three ships, three brigs and eight smaller vessels.

Once the soldiers enter the town, they begin a rampage of atrocities and cruelties of a character more common to savages than to men. The houses of the citizens are given up as spoils to the conquerors with their pilfering hands and brutish outrages that carry terror to every heart. It makes Savannah a scene of anguish and distress.

The citizens can only stand and stare in horror as they witness the defending patriots fleeing before the victorious onslaught of the enemy. An enemy that marches in with rolling drums and flying colors and a thirst for blood and spoils made keener by victory.

The Highlanders rip open feather beds with their bayonets and destroy public papers and records and allow them to blow about in the streets with the other debris.

Savannah Under Siege

Even a German Hessian officer serving with the British says, "it's a pity." The finest furnishings along with mahogany tables and chairs are literally smashed and thrown in the streets.

British soldiers are ruthless as they pursue the shattered American forces through the town. Many of the fleeing patriots are bayoneted and even some civilians in the town who are not agile enough to get out of their way. The troops are beyond bloodthirsty as they plunge their bayonets repeatedly into the sides of the retreating Americans until upon withdrawing their blades, they relish in extracting their victim's entrails.

The troops enter the streets of the town with their hands and bayonets dripping with the blood of Savannah's husbands, fathers, brothers and sons. Their faces are begrimed with sweat, dust and gunpowder and their countenances are glowering with rage and a pent-up lust chaffing to be let loose upon the vanquished.

Upon the capture of Savannah Col. Innes, who is aide-de-camp to Sir Henry Clinton and has accompanied the expedition, is assigned the immediate command of the town. The Americans captured are given the choice of either joining the British loyalists or being sent to one of the prison ships in the river. Most refuse to fight for the British and become victims on the prison ships where they are subjected to the most cruel and inhuman treatment imaginable.

They are crowded together in deplorable conditions and tyrannized by every petty officer. The food on these ships consists of condemned pork and oatmeal that is so rat infested that even the swine on board ignore it. Even so, the prisoners are still stinted in provisions along with every necessity of life and treated with such savage barbarity that four or more are dying every day. When this occurs their bodies are thrown into the marsh where they are eaten by the buzzards and crows at their leisure. Once on these ships, brutal treatment combined with disease dispatches most prisoners in only a few months.

Numbering among the prisoners is Jonathan Bryan, longtime Georgia patriot, who is in the waning part of his life. Though elderly, Bryan sets a stalwart example as a prisoner that many of the younger men would do well to emulate. His son James is also captured. They were taken from his plantation upriver at Brampton (near town of Garden City) when the British were actually looking for his son-in-law John Houstoun, then governor of Georgia. Bryan's wife is left to manage the farm. His daughter pleads on his behalf with the officers in charge and is rewarded with lewd and common treatment.

With very little effort the British have killed or drowned eighty-three and captured four hundred and fifteen non-commissioned officers and privates along with thirty-eight officers, forty-eight cannons, twenty-three mortars, ninety-four barrels of gunpowder plus the fort overlooking the river with all its stores. In short, they now have the capital of Georgia with all its shipping and large quantities of provisions.

Years later Gen. Henry "Light-Horse Harry" Lee would write, "never, has a victory of such magnitude been so completely gained with so little loss." The British losses amount to only three killed and ten wounded. Campbell says of his conquest of Savannah, "I may venture to say I have ripped one star and one stripe from the rebel flag of America."

Howe, with the remnants of his small army, camps for the night at Cherokee Hill about eight miles upriver from the town. On the following day he retreats even farther to Zubley's Ferry and crosses into South Carolina at Purysburg. There, a few days later, he meets with Gen. Lincoln, his new commander and is formally relieved of his command. Lincoln reaches Purysburg on the 3rd of January, five days after the fall of Savannah.

Savannah Under Siege

Lincoln Takes Command

Almost eight hundred Americans, the majority of the force assigned to defend the state, have been killed, wounded or captured. The British are in effective control of the eastern part of Georgia. Sir James Wright, the Royal Governor who had been formally deposed by the patriots, is again declared governor of Georgia. He re-establishes himself in the governor's mansion in Savannah where earlier he had been held captive. Bullet marks on the exterior of the house are still in evidence where his captors fired at the building while he and his family were inside.

From his place in refuge, the patriot governor, John Houstoun, pens a hasty note to Gen. Lincoln saying that the day has been lost. The British are again in control of Savannah. From that moment on, the destruction of the British base at Savannah is the objective of first priority for the American military in the South.

The American army calls for a court of inquiry into Gen. Howe's performance. Although he is cleared, his career as a field commander is over. He alone has to bear the blame for attempting to make a stand with untried troops when facing superior numbers. Apparently, the test of his abilities on the field of Mars proved him far less equal to his prior successes with Venus. By hindsight, the obvious strategy would have been to withdraw from the city and join forces with Lincoln, strengthen the army and then return to retake Savannah.

Col. Campbell issues a proclamation hoping to encourage the town's citizens to submit and support the Royal government. They are required to take an oath of allegiance to the King in order to come under British protection. In large numbers the Georgians relent and take advantage of this promise of amnesty. They soon discover if they decline, the alternative is to find their homes pilfered and their families threatened, enduring terror night and day.

H. Ronald Freeman

Their personal effects are taken; their children sometimes slain in front of them in their yards, their livestock either slaughtered or driven off, their crops destroyed and their houses burned. Others, now that the despised Tories are in control, move either to the northwestern part of the state, away from Tory retribution and the British government, or across the river into Carolina.

The roads leading out of Savannah teem with American sympathizers fleeing the British. This wall of human misery steadily trudges along sandy roads carrying their few possessions or trundling along behind pushcarts and wheelbarrows. They know not where they are going and only that it must be "away" from the certainty of punishment by the British.

In warfare, ancient or modern, it is always difficult to convey the human anguish and distress of noncombatants. The interest from a historic standpoint is in battles and campaigns and often overlooked is the unending tale of burned or pillaged homes. This, combined with the accompanying hunger, filth, wretchedness, anxiety, loss of property and breakup of families produced a feeling of total abandonment.

At the outbreak of the war and with the signing of the Declaration of Independence, Americans were firmly in control of their property. However, in two short years, the British regain control of the city. With that, things are reversed and the loyalists are rewarded with the confiscated property of the Americans. This is done in a clever legal maneuver by listing the former American owner and the present Tory claimant in the *Royal Georgia Gazette* and asking each to present his claim. The American, of course, does not dare return to Savannah. In his absence, the property is forfeited and subsequently awarded to the Tory.

After his capture of Sunbury, Gen. Prevost moves

up to Savannah and joins with Col. Campbell. It is January 1779. Now, Prevost, having been promoted to major general, assumes command of the combined forces, establishing his headquarters in Savannah, and sends Campbell north up the Savannah River to take Augusta. On his way Campbell occupies the small settlement of Ebenezer about 25 miles from Savannah. This is on January 2nd and is made with almost no resistance.

Ebenezer becomes a gathering point for the British. It is where all prisoners are taken who are captured in the surrounding area. From there they are ultimately escorted to Savannah. As Campbell approaches Augusta it too is taken with very little effort and is in British possession by January 29th. At this point, Georgia's patriot forces are totally disbursed and the state is wholly in British hands.

The primary American camp moves upriver to Purysburg, which is on the Carolina side. The American troops are strong enough to defend against an attack but not strong enough to initiate one. Although in dominance, the British soon discover it is one thing to rout outnumbered and ill trained soldiers but quite another to preserve control in areas not actually occupied by British soldiers. Prevost moves the majority of his army, numbering three thousand troops and an unknown number of Tory irregulars, up to Ebenezer. There, the two armies, separated only by the swampy barrier of the Savannah River, face each other.

Two heroes to emerge from this period are Sgt. William Jasper and his companion, Sgt. John Newton. They are both serving with the 2nd Continental Regiment of South Carolina and are acting as independent scouts for the American army. Jasper has already distinguished himself at Fort Sullivan near Charleston when the fort was actively engaged and being fired upon by British warships.

As the guns poured shells into the fort, one shot took down the flagstaff bearing the Carolina blue flag with a white crescent. All day it had waved defiantly during the onslaught and let observers watching from the roofs in Charleston know that their men still held the British at bay. When the flagstaff shattered, so did the hopes of a multitude of patriots.

It did not lie in the hot sand for long. Sgt. Jasper, a young Georgian, jumped from the fort in the face of deadly fire, walked the entire length in full view of the British, and then cut the flag from its pole. Climbing the wall, he called for a cannon sponge-staff to which he fastened the flag and again planted it on the wall. The onlookers from both sides were amazed at his courage.

For his heroism Jasper was presented a sword by Gov. John Rutledge, whose younger brother Edward had been a signer of the Declaration of Independence from South Carolina. He was also offered a commission in the continental army. He graciously accepted the sword but declined the commission. Jasper felt his lack of education would be an embarrassment to him in his attempt to command men. Instead he accepted an appointment as a free roaming scout, a position that suited him most ably.

It is said that Jasper is a master of disguise and can slip in and out of enemy lines undetected, securing valuable information as he goes. Neither does it hurt that his brother is a British loyalist and is camped with the British at Ebenezer. As he and Sgt. Newton visit his brother one evening, they notice a family that is being held among the prisoners. Their name is Jones. They are waiting to be escorted to Savannah on the following day for execution. Jasper and Newton visit briefly with the prisoners and they vow to themselves to do whatever possible to thwart British plans.

The next morning, Jasper and Newton follow the guard detail back to Savannah. Knowing they will probably stop at a spring just outside the city, they skirt around the detail and hide in the bushes at the spring and wait. They guessed right and before long they hear the approach of the small entourage of prisoners. The guards dismount and actually stack their muskets while they relax at the spring. Suddenly Jasper and Newton spring from the woods killing two of the guards and holding the others at gunpoint. The prisoners are freed and cross the river to the protection of the American camp at Purysburg. It is one of many exploits that are told and retold about Jasper around patriot campfires.

*　　*　　*　　*　　*　　*　　*　　*　　　*

Benjamin Lincoln is selected by Congress in the autumn of 1778 to take command of the American military efforts in the South. Even George Washington had recommended him, based on his effective use of the militia in the north. A friendship and mutual respect had developed between Lincoln and Washington during the siege of Boston.

His unclear diction, filled with New England colloquialisms, is strange to Carolina ears. When he is his usual humorous self, few men are any kinder or more engaging than Lincoln. He is sometimes criticized as being overcautious since he makes no important decisions without first deliberating with his officers. While Lincoln may not excel as a strategist, there are few that are his equal when it comes to organizational skills. He is a tireless administrator who is scrupulously honest. Lincoln demonstrates industry, spirit, and patient good humor.

When the British fleet reached Savannah, Lincoln marched from Charleston as soon as he could to reinforce Gen. Howe. Since the governor of South Carolina was more concerned about the threat to his state, Lincoln was only able to muster two regiments of Charleston militia. Therefore, he depended primarily on the newly arrived North Carolina continentals. With his small force and late start he had to be realistic about his military objectives. He knew if he was too late to save Savannah, he would have to work to prevent the British from extending their influence into the lower South.

When Lincoln neared within thirty miles of the town, he was informed of Campbell's victory over Howe's vastly outnumbered force. He considered his options and decided to station his army as close to the enemy as possible but in keeping with safety. In line with this thinking, he headed for Purysburg, about twenty-three miles upriver from the British held city but on the Carolina side.

Although Lincoln receives reinforcements from the remnants of Howe's decimated army, his total force is so depleted from militia desertions that it only numbers about fourteen hundred men. Within this body the majority are still militia who are not adequately disciplined for battle. At the same time, Georgia loyalists are flocking to the British camps and are making peace at the expense of patriotism.

Prevost, at his new command post in Savannah, thinks his troops will receive the same loyalist reception they did in Georgia from South Carolina residents. In pursuing this reasoning he orders two hundred men to march on Beaufort, about thirty miles to the east of Lincoln's position. He wants to get an idea of the lay of the land and assess the degree of British sentiment in the rural areas of Carolina.

By this time North Carolina continental's as well as additional militia have reinforced Lincoln. It brings his troop strength to about thirty-six hundred. When he learns of the British detachment moving on Beaufort, he dispatches three hundred South Carolina militia under Gen. Moultrie to confront them. Militia troops are anxious to make a showing in their home state. After a hotly contested but brief engagement, the small British expedition is forced to flee back to Savannah by sea. Moultrie and the militia conduct themselves proudly against the British regulars.

Moultrie is a South Carolinian who had been a member of the provincial congress at the outbreak of the revolution. He sided with the patriot cause and took command of a fort he had built of sand and palmetto logs on Sullivan's Island off Charleston. He was able to defend the fort successfully against heavy British attack in June 1777 and it was named Fort Moultrie in his honor. It was in that battle that Sgt. Jasper rescued the flag while under heavy fire. Moultrie received the thanks of Congress and is promoted to brigadier general in the continental Army.

H. Ronald Freeman

Kettle Creek

By this time Campbell is in occupation of Augusta. Operating nearby, a young American colonel named John Dooley has collected a small army of a few hundred patriots. His group is actively engaged with a comparable force of citizens who have remained loyal to the Crown. The loyalists are successful in driving Dooley into Carolina where he is reinforced by Col. Andrew Pickens of South Carolina, giving them a combined force of about five hundred and fifty men. Dooley is the senior officer but waives command in favor of Pickens, who commands more men.

The patriots receive word that the Tory leader, Col. James Boyd and his infamous "Bandits" are in the area. Boyd is a Tory agent recently sent into South Carolina to recruit 6,000 loyalist volunteers. He has just returned from a meeting in New York with British commander Henry Clinton. Only 600 men are actually raised. Boyd's failure to enlist anywhere near the expected numbers of loyalists reveals the major flaw in Britain's southern strategy, that of overestimating American enthusiasm for the royal cause. Many Tory recruits join only out of fear or intimidation.

The pillaging by this group throughout the countryside has created a lasting bitterness among the patriots. Like plundering marauders, Boyd's Bandits appropriate property for their own use, abuse the citizens, and even butcher several who dare to oppose their demands. Campbell in Augusta awaits Boyd's arrival.

It is said that no virtuous woman can be shielded from the Bandits' treacherous brutality and not even the most humble cottages escape their torches. No wonder that the history of these stormy times is replete with hatred for the citizen loyalists who did these things. That same hatred is not felt for the soldiers of the King, even though many bitter feelings are awakened by the red coated soldiers of George III.

Dooley and Pickens plan to intercept Boyd at Cherokee Ford about thirty miles above Augusta. Boyd, learning of this, attempts to escape across the ford. In his path is a blockhouse manned by an American lieutenant and eight men. The house is fortified with two heavy rotating guns. They refuse his crossing and force him to cross on rafts about five miles farther to the north.

Due to the delay, a detachment from the patriots' group overtakes Boyd and crosses the river before him and waits. Boyd and his troops cross the river at different points so as to deceive the patriots who are following. He is intercepted by the detachment of about a hundred men led by Capt. Anderson. They have been watching his movements and are in fact able to guess correctly the point on the river where Boyd's Bandits will cross. As the crossing is underway, the patriots ambush them from a canebrake.

Anderson places his troops under concealment in the canebrake and pours a destructive fire into Boyd's main body as they cross the river. Some of Boyd's troops have crossed higher upriver and sizing up the situation are able to flank behind Anderson's small party and compel his retreat back to where he rejoins Pickens and Dooley. During the short, bitter struggle, Boyd loses over a hundred men killed or wounded to only a few for the Americans. After the battle, Boyd proceeds on into Georgia just ahead of Pickens and the balance of his force.

Boyd's band rides west, intent on joining with Col. Daniel McGirth who is expected to meet him about six miles away at a spot on Little River. McGirth leads a Tory force of about five hundred men. The plan is for the combined group to join Campbell in Augusta.

Immediately after crossing the river, Boyd feels he is safe and is unaware that Dooley and Pickens have continued in pursuit. Col. Elijah Clarke has further reinforced the Americans with a body of one hundred mounted cavalry. This united force crosses the river shortly after Boyd and pursues rapidly but cautiously. They make camp within four miles of their opponent's encampment. From there they can hear the beat of enemy drums and know based on smoldering fires from the Tories, they aren't far ahead.

Boyd has crossed the Savannah River on February 14th, a month and a half after the fall of Savannah, and halts on a farm near Kettle Creek. He makes camp and turns his horses out to forage among the reeds in a nearby canebrake and relaxes his security for the evening. He has no reason to suspect the near proximity of the Americans. His men butcher several of the farmer's fat steers and then scatter to gather wood to cook the meat and parch corn. Boyd camps on open ground with a creek behind, a canebrake on each flank and farmland in the front. His army is dispersed in various directions.

The patriots prepare for battle once again and again they are at a great disadvantage in numbers to the Tories. This time they are outnumbered almost two to one. They count on pluck and surprise to hopefully give them a victory and prevent Boyd from joining Campbell's British garrison at Augusta. At stake is no less than the supremacy of upper Georgia. Much depends on this battle and the patriots know it.

If Boyd's forces are successful in driving the Americans back, British loyalists can rest assured that for a long time; no further resistance from the patriots will follow. All civilians will then yield to British power. On the other hand, should the Americans prevail, it will not only crush Tory power, already so galling to the patriots, but also protect them from further insult. It will also stimulate American courage, which is especially necessary, since it is at a low ebb after a long series of disasters. It is a big moment indeed for the fate of upper Georgia.

Savannah Under Siege

The Americans emerge quickly from the woods and swoop down upon Boyd's pickets. The first notice of attack is given by a volley from the pickets as they open fire on the Americans rapidly drawing near. The American troops have been ordered not to fire until they are within at least thirty-five paces of the enemy. In the excitement of the moment they disobey their orders and return fire.

Boyd's camp is startled by the sudden sound of rifle fire and initially swarms in a state of confusion. Still, they attempt to rally and mount a defense. The American army advances steadily with the right flank under Dooley, the left under Elijah Clark and Pickens commanding the center. There are about a hundred men on each flank and two hundred in the center. Boyd is able to gather and deploy about a hundred of his men behind a fence that is filled in with fallen timbers. From there he has a good vantagepoint.

Observing this half formed abatis (barricade), Pickens files off to the right to a rise in the ground. From this position he is able to flank Boyd, rushing down upon him as he flees. Reacting to Pickens flanking movement, Boyd orders his men to fall back and unite with the main force. During this retreat, Col. Boyd is mortally wounded with three musket balls in his body; two through the chest and one in the leg.

Clarke and Dooley both have been impeded in their advances while picking their way through the canebrakes. After slow progress, they are finally united again with the center and bloody fighting ensues over the entire field. The loyalists, now under the command of Maj. Spurgeon, begin to give ground. They fall back across the creek leaving behind many firearms, horses and baggage.

To the rear is a small hill that Clarke is quick to recognize as a point that will undoubtedly be chosen by the Tories as a rallying ground. He discovers a path leading to a ford across the creek where he will be able to pursue.

H. Ronald Freeman

Ordering his men to follow, Clarke spurs his horse forward and it is immediately shot from beneath him. Promptly, he remounts and dashes through the water, but with only about a quarter of his force. He seizes one side of the hill as the loyalists take possession of the other. Clarke follows a circuitous route and emerges on the other side of the hill in the rear of Spurgeon. The enemy is now hemmed in on both sides. Pickens and Dooley press forward and the fighting is continued with renewed vigor.

The battle continues for almost two confused hours that sees the combatants break into smaller skirmishes and even individual encounters. The fighting is hand to hand with bayonets, rifle butts and fists. At last the Tories gave way in confusion and flee from the field, a routed and defeated force. Never again will Boyd's Bandits assemble as an organized body during the remainder of the war. The encounter, though small, is savage and its aftermath is one of bitter recrimination.

As Boyd lies dying, he says he left Carolina with eight hundred men and has lost about a hundred who have been killed, wounded or deserted in crossing the river. In this skirmish the Tories have lost seventy men killed, seventy-five wounded and a like number captured. The Americans have lost nine killed and about twenty wounded. The Tories also lose six or seven hundred horses as well as the greater part of their baggage and stores.

Boyd dies during the night and is buried on the battlefield. He gives Col. Pickens his articles of value consisting of a broach, a watch, his sword and spurs and asks that they be forwarded to his wife in England with a letter explaining the manner of his death. He says to tell her that his last thoughts are of her and his last prayer is for her welfare. Pickens sees that his wishes are carried out.

The Americans camp that night a short distance from the battlefield near where the town of Washington, Georgia stands today. The prisoners are taken to South

Carolina and tried for treason. Five of their leaders are hanged. When McGirth hears about Boyd's defeat, he retreats at once to Augusta and joins Col. Campbell.

Kettle Creek is minor in terms of the number of troops involved but it has a marked impact on subsequent events along the Georgia-South Carolina border. It represents the first real victory for the patriots in many weeks. This gives a new spirit to the cause and takes the wind from the sails of the Tories, who lose much of their confidence.

The British have gone to great lengths to convince the loyalists to go to arms in support of the Crown and that they would be there when they needed protection from the patriots. The small skirmish at Kettle Creek reveals to the Tories that British assurances are indeed empty. As a result the loyalists soon become dispersed all over the region. Some run to North Carolina and some just run. Others return home and cast themselves on the mercy of the new American government.

H. Ronald Freeman

Briar Creek

Gen. Lincoln is distressed by Campbell's penetration to Augusta since he receives most of his supplies from the Augusta area. Also, he wants to discourage the loyalists from further assisting the British and to this end decides to initiate an offensive. His army has been strengthened by hundreds of militiamen. They have been drawn to his camp after Moultrie's victory at Beaufort gives them renewed hope.

Lincoln dispatches Gen. John Ashe of North Carolina up the Savannah River with fifteen hundred of his home state militia along with several companies of Georgia continentals. The proposed plan seems to be for him to join Gen. Andrew Williamson and his nearly one thousand troops for a combined attack on Augusta. In reality, Ashe has no immediate orders to attack since Lincoln knows that he will soon lose some four hundred militia from expiring enlistments.

On the British side, Campbell has received word from McGirth of Boyd's rout at Kettle Creek and fearing he will be trapped in Augusta, withdraws immediately and heads for the protection of Savannah. Gen. Lincoln orders Ashe to cross the Savannah River into Georgia and pursue Campbell as far as Briar Creek, about forty-five miles below Augusta. Back in Savannah, Prevost is quite concerned by the American resistance at Kettle Creek and the exposed position of Campbell near Augusta. He knows Lincoln's army at Purysburg is growing daily.

Col. Campbell has already proven himself when he routed the patriots at Savannah, as both clever and dangerous. Here we have a seasoned military man facing a politically appointed general. When Campbell learns of the proposed concentration of American forces, he determines to strike at what he thinks is the weakest point of the enemy, that being the position of Ashe at Briar

Creek.   Here, about fifty miles above Savannah, Campbell is given a rare opportunity to turn on his pursuers.

He crosses the creek at Hudson's Ferry from the north and destroys the bridge behind him.   Knowing that Ashe's army will be detained at the remnants of the bridge, he dispatches Prevost's younger brother, Lt. Col. Marc Prevost, on an encircling movement.   This requires a fifty-mile march around the American flank.   Though difficult, Col. Prevost executes it with precision.   He is required to re-cross Briar Creek, fifteen miles behind the American position.   The bridge there has been severed and his troops have a problem in crossing the swollen creek. Eventually though, they pass over on pontoons.   His detachment is only a few miles from the American rear when he is detected.

As Ashe approaches the destroyed bridge at Hudson's Ferry he orders it repaired and then personally recrosses the Savannah River back into Carolina to confer with Lincoln.   Lincoln has called for a council of war comprised of generals Moultrie, Ashe and Rutherford.   The council has been assembled for the purpose of again discussing the uniting of all patriot forces into one army.

There is concern expressed to Ashe by his fellow generals about his position at Briar Creek.   He is questioned about it specifically.   He replies he is confident in his ability to hold his own against any force the enemy can bring against him.   He only asks that a detachment with two pieces of artillery be sent to him.   Gen. Lincoln complies immediately.

When Ashe returns to his Georgia encampment, he discovers the repair of the bridge has barely begun.   Also, little has been done to prepare his troops to either attack or set up a defensive operation.   His small army is in the angle formed by Briar Creek and its surrounding marsh and the Savannah River.

His camp is set between the deep, swollen and

impassable creek on its left, the Savannah River in its rear with no boat to cross it, a lagoon deep and wide on its right and facing an open uninterrupted entrance for the enemy on its front. Col. Prevost, seeing Ashe's plight, moves rapidly to engage the Americans. Advance warnings fail to reach Ashe and as a consequence his unsuspecting troops are totally surprised on the afternoon of February 28th.

The Americans have two problems. First, the troops are scattered and secondly, the individual soldiers have no ammunition. Why? The American's have a practice of carrying their shot and powder under their arms and in their shirts and in the past, much ammunition has been ruined during their marching. To avoid this, Gen. Ashe decided to collect the ammunition and distribute it only prior to an engagement.

At the outset of the unexpected attack, precious time is forfeited and confusion reigns because the soldiers need to receive ammunition when they should be forming their line of battle. Not only that, the troops are outfitted with many different weapons. Some carry rifles, some shotguns, others muskets, and a few are put in the lines with nothing but clubs. Arming them is difficult and time consuming since they all have different weapons.

Retreat is impossible given the surrounding terrain. American officers form their men as hurriedly as they can and begin to proceed toward the enemy. Col. Samuel Elbert and Col. Andrew Pickens lead the advance. Lt. Col. John McIntosh, of Fort Morris at Sunbury fame, serves with Elbert. The British form their line about one hundred and fifty yards from the Americans.

Primary on the British front are the 71st Highlanders and the corps of light infantry under Sir James Baird. The Americans open with a heavy fire. After a few volleys the Georgians begin a movement to the left and the North Carolina troops behind them move to the right. This creates a noticeable gap in the American lines. The British move quickly to exploit the error.

It is too much for the North Carolinians. Their Halifax Regiment scampers off without firing a shot. The Wilmington Regiment is somewhat better. It advances, fires a few volleys then turns and retreats to the almost impassable barrier of the swamp and creek. The New Bern and Edmonton regiments do the same and before long, all North Carolina units are in full flight, throwing down their arms and gear as they flee.

Ashe tries his best to rally the troops. Fortunately, the Georgia continentals, his best-trained troops, hold their ground. In fact, Samuel Elbert and John McIntosh put up such a fight the British have to call up their reserves. Even greatly outnumbered, the Georgians continue fighting until every avenue of retreat is cut off. Finally at last, Elbert is forced to surrender and retire what remains of his men. With the flight of the North Carolinians, their flanks have collapsed and make it possible for the British to move in and surround them.

Col. Elbert, along with most of his men, is taken prisoner. He is lined up with the other captured Americans and upon being recognized, is struck down by a British soldier. The British treatment of prisoners here is much like their cruelty in the aftermath of the capture of Savannah. Elbert remembers that well and is at the point of being skewered by an uplifted bayonet when he makes the Masonic sign of distress. A British officer nearby, recognizing the sign, restrains the arm of the soldier and spares Elbert's life.

Many others at Briar Creek are not so lucky and the same type of British massacre that had occurred at Savannah proceeds as before. While many of the patriots are on their hands and knees praying for quarter, British troops are engaging with relish in what today would be considered war crimes of the most barbarous nature.

Most of the bodies of American troops are disfigured

beyond recognition by repeated gashes and stab wounds. Capt. Baird of the 71st Highlanders takes a lead in personally executing about a dozen of the supplicating Americans. Earlier, Baird shouted to his men during the American rout, "any man who takes a prisoner will lose his ration of rum."

The broken ranks of Americans escape the best way they can; it's every man for himself. Some are slogging through the bog and others are attempting to swim the river. Unfortunately, many can't and drown or are killed by the British; one hundred and fifty by rough count. Prisoners number close to two hundred along with captured American artillery and supplies plus five hundred muskets and rifles. British losses are small; one officer killed and fifteen privates killed or wounded. Gen. Ashe is discovered about two miles down river among his troops, swimming to safety.

What is most surprising at Briar Creek is not the British victory, which in retrospect everything favored. The advantages are easy to tick off. Their army was larger, they had the element of surprise and the Americans lacked any plan of retreat. It is also obvious that the British troops reflected vastly superior discipline and training. Still, the startling disparity in the casualties between the two forces is difficult to understand. The Americans are reputed to be fine marksmen. If they have over one thousand troops engaged and even a third of them fire at close range, casualties should be far heavier than the sixteen killed or wounded on the British side.

The battle of Briar Creek becomes one of the most disastrous setbacks for the Americans in the war. Both Gen. Lincoln and Gen. Ashe are subjected to severe criticism. It is felt Lincoln used poor judgement in dividing his small force. The critics also question his placing troops under the command of an officer in whose judgment and skill he is not totally confident.

Ashe is a political general, an appointment gained

through being a good patriot. Unfortunately, this in no way equates with being a competent soldier. He was weak in reconnaissance and in securing his post. He should never have left his command to go confer with Lincoln until he was satisfied his camp was secure. Also, he knew he was operating in an area where a surprise encounter with the enemy was always a possibility. In light of this, he ran the unacceptable risk of not giving his soldiers an adequate supply of ammunition.

Ashe also misused his militia. How? It is a military fact that the greatest advantage of militia is its speed and mobility. By lingering for three days at Briar Creek, he sacrificed both of these. His delay allowed Campbell the opportunity to devise tactics for his defeat and Col. Prevost the time to execute them. Ashe is so widely criticized that he requests his own court-martial. Overall, he is fortunate. Gen. Moultrie presides over the Court of Inquiry. As a result of that trial, Ashe is cleared of charges of cowardice and inefficiency but is blamed for failing to take proper security measures.

The defeat at Briar Creek totally erases the meager psychological gain the Americans realized by their victory at Kettle Creek, only two weeks earlier. It raises Tory morale and opens a line of communication among the British, Tories and Indians. Probably the biggest lesson to be learned from Briar Creek is that there is no substitute for military training and experience. What is an automatic course of action to career British officers usually does not even occur to the American generals. The lessons for the armies in the South are hard and painful. It is said of Lincoln that his stock of military knowledge is not considerable. It is also agreed that when he acquires that knowledge, it is at a great cost. Indeed Briar Creek is an expensive lesson.

After Briar Creek, Lincoln abandons all hope of recovering Georgia. It can be argued in defense of Ashe, that few patriot generals could have done better in the face of such an able and daring enemy attack. Lincoln shoulders his share of the blame and informs Congress that he is be willing to resign his southern command. The only good thing to come out of the Briar Creek debacle is that Col. Campbell is ordered back to England. On March 11th, he returns on the man-of-war *Phoenix.*

As a result of the Briar Creek disaster, Gov. John Rutledge of South Carolina begins to doubt that Lincoln can defend his state against the British. He initiates his own course of action and begins stationing most of the new militia recruits in the Charleston, Augusta and Orangeburg garrisons. In fact, in Orangeburg in the center of the state, he personally places himself in command of three thousand militia.

Gradually, new recruits join Lincoln and he feels his forces are of sufficient strength to protect Augusta. It is important since that's where the Georgia legislature is about to convene. Lincoln leaves with four thousand men and marches toward Augusta. He orders most of his remaining men to reposition about ten miles upriver to an area called Black Swamp, still below Augusta. He hopes that by establishing an additional post on the river, he can deter the British from crossing at a weak point into Carolina. These troops will be under the command of Gen. Moultrie. Lincoln feels this small contingent will secure South Carolina from attack. Considering Prevost's vast majority of British forces near the coast, it is an unrealistic assumption.

Lincoln is practically inviting an attack by leaving Moultrie with such a small force. He leaves orders with Moultrie that if the British attack and begin a move toward Charleston, he should fight a delaying action as much as possible to give Lincoln's army time to come up and reinforce him. In effect, Lincoln is placing Charleston in jeopardy - the very city he has been charged by Gov. Rutledge to defend.

H. Ronald Freeman

Charleston and Stono Ferry

When Gen. Prevost learns the American forces have been scattered across Carolina, he is confident that with five thousand men at his disposal, he can overrun the state. In April, Prevost, to counter Lincoln's move to Augusta, crosses the river at Purysburg with twenty-five hundred men. At that point he initiates a chess match, waiting for Lincoln's countermove. He knows Lincoln will not allow him to advance on Charleston unopposed.

Lincoln feels Prevost is bluffing and crosses the river with his army into Georgia and marches toward Savannah to threaten its token British garrison. Lincoln assumes the British move is only made as a distraction to divert him. His line of march carries him in the general direction of Charleston so he can keep the option open of supporting that city if necessary.

Gen. Prevost however does not take the bait and continues his steady procession toward Charleston. Although Prevost has no specific plans to attack that city, since he encounters almost no opposition, he begins advancing up the coast behind Moultrie's retreating troops. Along the way, the British continue to pillage and loot in what has become a familiar part of their strategy.

Lincoln learns almost too late that Moultrie was unable to halt the invaders and is retreating toward Charleston. At last he has become alert to the threat. He acknowledges the failure of his feint toward Savannah and crosses the river once more in pursuit of the British. Rapidly, the chess match is reaching end game and the race for Charleston is on.

Gov. Rutledge joins in and rushes east from Orangeburg with his militia to strengthen the capital city. Lincoln combines with the others in tightening the ring with their convergence on Charleston. Prevost's forces are intent on looting the coastal plantations and in so doing are allowing precious time for the city to strengthen its defenses.

Prevost finally moves his troops into position but dawdles for three days when his force is within striking distance of the city. He is receiving confusing reports that suggest Lincoln might be on the point of attacking Savannah with a large force. While Prevost waits for clarification, Charleston receives substantial reinforcements from Gov. Rutledge, coming in from Orangeburg.

On May 11th the British stand before the city and demand its immediate surrender. It appears the city fathers and businessmen are more attuned to the welfare of their pocketbooks than in defending the patriot cause. As such, the leading merchants and planters are in total despair for their safety and even more so for the protection of their property. Gen. Lincoln is still in transit and no one really knows when to expect him. The town's influential citizens pressure Gov. Rutledge to pledge the neutrality of South Carolina for the duration of the war if the British will spare the city. Rutledge reluctantly agrees.

Surprisingly, Prevost rejects the offer. His scouts have informed him that Lincoln with a large force is approaching from the south and is near the British rear. He feels he has little alternative now but to withdraw to the coastal islands and prepare for an evacuation by sea.

Prevost's scouts intercept a message from Gen. Lincoln to Gen. Moultrie assuring him that he is making for Charleston as quickly as possible. To avoid Lincoln's army, Prevost moves east toward the sea islands near Charleston. There, not more than three miles from the city, he waits to be supplied by vessels from New York.

If Lincoln had arrived earlier, he might have trapped the British between a tightening American vise. However, Lincoln is in no hurry to attack the British even though they are backed up to the coast. He is getting little assistance since Gov. Rutledge will not lend reinforcements from his troops in the city, fearing it will render them vulnerable to another enemy attack.

Prevost establishes a strong defensive position at the Stono Ferry on the mainland side of the Stono River, across from Johns Island. It is from that island that the British plan to embark on the boats which will carry them back to Savannah. Col. Maitland and nine hundred British regulars and German Hessians have been stationed at the ferry to secure Prevost's main corridor of retreat. About six hundred additional British troops get set to embark from Johns Island.

Lincoln moves his primary camp to about six miles north of Stono Ferry. He dispatches eight hundred South Carolina militiamen to James Island, adjacent to Johns Island. These are under the command of Gen. Moultrie. Their mission is one of creating an impending threat to British forces under Prevost on Johns Island. It is planned as a diversion but Lincoln emphasizes to Moultrie that it is imperative that he prevent Prevost from reinforcing Maitland.

With Moultrie in place, Lincoln marches south to Stono Ferry and there positions his forces in the woods opposite the fortified British position. At daybreak the following morning, the battle erupts into furious hand-to-hand combat with the Americans driving the enemy back. The American detachment is substantial, numbering over a thousand troops with half being continental regulars.

The British line is composed of the 71st Scottish Higlanders on the right and a Hessian regiment on the left. The 71st Regiment under Col. Maitland rushes out to cover the withdrawal of British pickets but is badly mauled by the continentals. Encouraged by this, and wishing to press the attack, Lincoln orders a bayonet charge.

The British hold their fire until the Americans are within about sixty yards and then release a combined barrage of artillery and musket fire. The patriots again go

Savannah Under Siege

against orders and stop to return fire rather than pressing on with the bayonet attack and reserving their fire. Chaos ensues and a general firefight erupts. When it seems the British will give way to increasing pressure from the North Carolina militia, Col. Maitland recognizes the threat and adroitly shifts his Highlanders to the left while leaving his reserve in place to fill the gap. With the line of the Scots stiffening, the Hessian officers are able to rally their troops who had fallen back and the British line is again intact.

The line saws back and forth and after about an hour of pitched battle neither side has an advantage. On nearby James Island Gen. Moultrie encounters a shortage of boats for crossing and is unable to deflect the British on Johns Island. This means Gen. Prevost can make full utilization of his forces in reinforcing Maitland. Lincoln observes Prevost's army marching toward the ferry and quickly orders a withdrawal. The retreat is lacking order and Maitland, attempting to seize the day, orders an attack by the entire force under his command.

Overzealous, the British like the patriots before them become too strung out and the American cavalry counterattacks them in turn. Again Maitland draws on his experience and quickly orders his men together behind a barrier of bayonets. It is standard formation for repelling cavalry by ground troops. The advancing horsemen also receive fire from Maitland's rear ranks. The charge is quickly aborted and the cavalry withdraw. Momentum swings again and the American militia is forced to retreat from a strong combined force of Hessians and Highlanders.

The retreating Americans are in danger of being overtaken and cut down. Suddenly, the Virginia brigade advances forward and renders a heavy fire. That halts the British pursuit and also allows the Americans to make their withdrawal. Lincoln is forced to withdraw back into the woods from whence he came. Patriot losses are about one hundred and fifty killed and wounded with the British casualties numbering about the same.

Lincoln admits that although he has not achieved the success he hoped for, he has shown his men that they can meet the enemy and beat them on equal grounds at any time.

Prevost withdraws his army via the inland waterway to Savannah and leaves Col. Maitland in command of the remaining force. They march southward and occupy Port Royal Island near Beaufort. Lincoln establishes his headquarters at nearby Sheldon. From there he can block any advances by land from Maitland.

As the British withdraw down the waterway toward Savannah their ships overflow with the loot from many months of pillaging the coastal plantations of Carolina. Since it was colonized earlier than Georgia, the plantations are much wealthier. They have barrels full of china and household furniture in large quantities. Raiding parties have visited almost every house, stripping the valuables then robbing any remaining inhabitants of their money, rings, jewelry and other personal ornaments. Burial vaults are broken open and bodies despoiled in the mad lust for possessions. What cannot be carried off is destroyed. Slaughtered livestock are left to rot in their own gore. Even cats and dogs are butchered in an orgy of destruction. The British are making their presence known.

Most of the coastal plantations are managed by paid overseers who have fled the retreating British. This only leaves the many black slaves, now without supervision. It is felt the rice fields are too hot and unhealthy for whites but the slaves are considered to be immune to malaria and other fevers and therefore are found on the coastal plantations in large numbers. There are probably fifteen thousand slaves on the coast of South Carolina during the Revolution. The slaves can either flee like the overseers or remain. Most choose to remain. With their masters absent, the slaves are all too eager to reveal to the British the

Savannah Under Siege

location of hidden treasures and become avid camp followers.

With the coming of the hot and humid summer season, neither the British nor the Americans have any interest of continuing campaigning until autumn. There is little for either side to do except prepare for the next campaign and attempt to preserve the health of the troops in this hostile climate. Gen. Lincoln orders all officers and soldiers to join their respective regiments and departs himself to take command of his army in Sheldon. He is again having difficulty in raising militia even though he increases their pay to equal that of the continental army.

H. Ronald Freeman

France to the Rescue

Gen. Lincoln and Gov. Rutledge of South Carolina, in a series of meetings in Charleston, weigh their options. They believe their best hope of saving that state and regaining Georgia depends on securing aid from their new allies, the French. They appeal to Admiral d'Estaing (destang), now operating in the West Indies, to join them in a unified Franco-American venture to dislodge the British from Georgia.

France has agreed to furnish critically needed military aid and loans to the American colonies. With her help, many think it can be the turning point of the Revolution. Resentful over the loss of its North American empire during the French and Indian War, France welcomed the opportunity to undermine Britain's position in the New World. Though it maintained a position of neutrality until 1777, France was quietly furnishing the colonists with munitions and loans. As early as 1776, America had been making overtures to seek recognition and financial aid from the Bourbon monarchy.

France has agreed with the Americans to renounce all claims to territories in North America east of the Mississippi River. The alliance greatly facilitates U.S. independence. The French fleet proceeds to challenge British control of North American waters and, together with troops and arms, is proving to be an indispensable asset in America's struggle.

D'Estaing is desirous of glory and easily enticed by the invitation. To capture Savannah would be a feat of arms that would far outshine his victories in the West Indies. It would also place the new republic of America under a never-ending obligation to its French allies. The victory would rank second only to the surrender of British General Bourgoyne at Saratoga. D'Estaing feels after Savannah capitulates, it will be followed by the surrender of

Savannah Under Siege

Col. Maitland at Beaufort. Superiority of equipment and numbers will be with the French and the Americans.

The Americans suggest that he consider sailing north in late summer when the danger of hurricanes makes operations in the Indies impracticable. D'Estaing likes the suggestion since it offers him an opportunity to make up for his failure at Newport in the preceding year. During that naval engagement he was forced to withdraw due to an unexpected storm. He was accused of cowardice by some Americans and is eager for the opportunity to redeem himself. The timeline for the expedition seems ideal and he concludes his Indies campaign in July with the capture of the British Island of Grenada. This places him in a confident mood and even though his fleet needs refitting, he sets sail for the coast of Georgia.

Upon arriving off the Georgia coast, d'Estaing sends an envoy of five ships to Charleston to let Gen. Lincoln know he is available and ready to cooperate in the capture of Savannah. At the same time he points out the necessity of a speedy campaign, since he cannot remain on the coast very long in the hurricane season of the year. Lincoln in turn dispatches boats to d'Estaing's fleet to assist in taking cannons and supplies to the shore.

Everyone's spirits rise since they are so sure of success. No one doubts the ability of the allied force to march to Savannah and do little more than demand surrender. A militia group has been formed and a multitude of volunteers eagerly join in order to be present at the surrender. They all want the first hand pleasure of seeing the British march out in humiliation and lay down their arms.

Not knowing the joint plans of the Americans and French, the British troops feel secure in Savannah. After all, haven't they taken it with very little effort and since then, defeated the Americans in almost every encounter?

H. Ronald Freeman

And then it happens. On September 8th, 1779, a courier awakens British Gov. Wright with a special dispatch from Gen. Prevost. The message confirms his worst fears. Sighted at anchor off Tybee Island are forty-two French ships of war, most of which appear to be very large. From the convergence of this fleet, there can be no doubt that an attack on Savannah is imminent. The first reaction of the British is both how and why?

Everyone believes Adm. d'Estaing's fleet is hundreds of miles away guarding France's rich possessions in the West Indies. Furthermore, why would he be the least interested in a small, poor American province? It is hard for Prevost to accept that Savannah could be the real French objective. It would be far more logical for d'Estaing to target Rhode Island or New York but here again, this is only conjecture. What is known is that the French are here. Many feel it could be for no better reason than avenging Britain's rape of their Bourbon Empire.

Savannah Under Siege

British Reaction

The British are totally unprepared for this sudden turn of events. Their forces are still divided. Although Prevost and a thousand men defend the town, Maitland's crack troops, who are the primary infantry force, are still garrisoned at Beaufort. Nine hundred men, comprising the 71st Regiment of Scotch Highlanders returned to that port after the battle of Stono Ferry only a few months before.

Even more distressing, the land route from Beaufort has been blocked by the Americans under Lincoln who are garrisoned at nearby Sheldon. By water, Beaufort is over fifty time consuming miles from Savannah. And now, the fleur-de-lis of France has risen up from the Caribbean and placed the cause of King George III in America, in jeopardy. Events for the British have indeed changed for the worse.

Another garrison of troops under New York loyalist Lt. Col. John Harris Cruger is stationed at Sunbury below Savannah. Cruger was mayor of New York City in 1764 and had sided with the British since the beginning of the war. His brother Nicholas in St. Croix had actually sponsored the education of the young patriot, Alexander Hamilton. Prevost immediately orders them back to Savannah as well as others at the outposts at Ebenezer, Ogeechee and Cherokee Hill. They are instructed to dismantle their forts, destroy what can't be carried and join the main body of the British army in Savannah.

On the 9th, the battery at Tybee near the lighthouse is destroyed, the guns spiked and the howitzer and stores carried back to Savannah. The small garrison is still able to fire on the French ships with their two guns but without effect. That night a French detachment occupies the fort, which they find abandoned.

Cruger comes in from Sunbury by land but sends his sick and infirmed on an armed vessel to come through the inland waterway. This is not to be. Contrary winds stall their passage until the enemy blockades the waterway. This forces them to change course to a new route through the Ogeechee River. On the night of October 1, the Americans intercept and prevent the detachment of British troops from reaching Savannah.

The British, under Captain French, have camped on the Ogeechee River. Col. John White, a Georgia continental with only two officers, a sergeant and three privates deceives the British captain into thinking a much larger force surrounds his camp. They light fires in the woods surrounding the camp, as if a whole army is bivouacked there; White demands the detachment surrender and the entire British command is taken prisoner.

The French flotilla is impressive. In all, they count twenty-two ships of the line, each hosting seventy-four guns or more. Additionally, there are ten frigates and smaller troop carriers with about four thousand men.

The fleet is strung out from Beaufort in the north to as far south as one can see from Tybee Light. Most are two deckers but some are of the triple-decker class. Many are older ships that have engaged in naval battles thirty years before. Others are newly constructed and Britain will have to deal with the power of their guns when Napoleon calls them back into service. Five ships are immediately dispatched to the mouth of the Savannah River to seal its entrance.

The warship names reflect the pride of France and melodiously roll from even the English tongue: *Annibal, Cesar, Dauphin Royal, Diademe, Fantasque, Fendant, Fier Rodrigue, Guerrier, Hector, Languedoc, Magnifique, Provence, Robuste, Sagittaire, Tonnant, Vaillant, Vengeur, and Zele* . Most of their officers are members of the nobility, which is typical of the French navy of the day. Even John Paul Jones, the American, has said that to be promoted from lieutenant to captain in the French

Savannah Under Siege

Navy, you must first produce proof of noble lineage going back at least four generations or otherwise be a member by birth of the order of the Chevalier of St. Louis.

The already famous admiral, Louis-Antoine de Bougainville, commands one of the vessels. Bougainville belongs to the faction of the French Navy known as "the blues" as distinguished from the "the reds". Being a "blue" distinguishes someone who has not entered the Navy on the lower rungs and subsequently made an orderly ascension through the grades, as did the "reds." Usually it was someone of noble birth or with political connections who was able to secure a commission as a ranking officer.

Still, Bougainville is one of the more interesting figures of his time. As a young man he had written a brilliant treatise on intregal calculus. After a short stint of reading law, he abandoned his practice for a profession in the military. He was able to secure the influence of Madame de Pompadour in becoming an aide who went on to serve with considerable distinction in Canada. Then, after a short career as a diplomat in London he successfully colonized the Falkland Islands off Argentina. Bougainville's name is most recognized as the source of the flaming tropical flower called Bougainvillea and a well-known island in the Solomon group.

The French plans are being formulated to land troops on a recommended location south of Savannah. Their longboats assemble near the *Languedoc,* d'Estaing's great flagship*.* These are filled with troops ready to make the journey a few miles up the coast for a landing. The boats are being sent to the plantation of Beaulieu on the Vernon River. It is there that d'Estaing has selected for the debarkation. The boats are crowded with as many as a hundred men in each.

One can imagine their discomfort in their uniforms of tight linen breeches with leggings that reach above the knee. Their necks are encircled with stiff collars which dress code regulations require to be hooked, even in the humid south.

Most of the soldiers wear broad cross belts to support heavy cartridge boxes along with tri-cornered hats. These are effective in shading their ears but not their eyes. Their hat is only one thing more to add to their misery. For the French foot soldier of the eighteenth century, his lot is bad enough under any circumstance. Many are not even known by their own name. Dissension pervades the ranks and most have been grumbling since they arrived on the Georgia coast. Everything seems delayed or confused. To add to their unhappy state, their commander-in-chief never seems quite certain what he is up to.

And let there be no doubt who is in command. It is Charles-Henri Comte d'Estaing, Vice Admiral of France and Lt. General of the Armies of the King. To look at his boyish complexion you would wonder that he could command anything. His face is almost feminine in its countenance. Conversely, this is certainly not true of his demeanor. The General is one who works tirelessly and seems to sleep for only a few hours a day. It has led to his habit of napping after dinner with his head resting upon his hands or sometimes lying down, but still fully clothed.

Although d'Estaing is a little over fifty years of age, his officers agree he possesses the fire of a man in his twenties. It has only been a few weeks before that he cut quite a gallant figure leading his troops at Grenada and cheering them forward with "Viva la Roi!" (Long Live the King).

D'Estaing's ancestor, Dieudonne d'Estaing, sacrificed his life to save King Philip Augustus at the battle of Bouvines in 1214. This heroic action entitled the d'Estaing family to wear the coat of arms of France. Also because of this, young Charles became a darling of the French court in early boyhood and continued into adulthood. John Paul Jones, the American naval captain who made several voyages to France has commented, "the King never had a subject who loved him better or who was a more worthy citizen."

Commanding a regiment as a colonel when he was only sixteen and yet a brigadier general at twenty-seven, d'Estaing is the model of the soldier and the idol of the seaman, but moral authority over his officers seems to escape him. He is brusque and autocratic in manner and is not particularly well thought of by many of his officers or men. However, his praise is lavish for the officers he deems to be deserving and he is tireless in his efforts to secure recognition for them.

In spite of personality problems, d'Estaing has garnered respect as a man of considerable intelligence as well as a tireless worker. As a fluent writer, he has composed poetry and will eventually write even a tragedy (*Les Thermopyles, 1791*). He is nothing less than brilliant. But d'Estaing has his troubled side as well.

He possesses the predominant foible of many of Marie Antoinette's courtiers. Most of his fortune has been squandered through gambling and high living, which has compelled his wife to bring litigation to separate her funds from his. There is also ample evidence that he is not a faithful husband. It is well known that d'Estaing is the father of a bastard son in Aukvergne and reputedly the sire of still another in Paris.

Beyond his personal failings, probably at the front of d'Estaing's faults is that he is extremely ambitious. His entire career has been marked with a long pursuit of personal advancement. General "Light Horse Harry" Lee will record scathingly in his journal that "no one is more obedient to the call of duty when it is connected with the prospect of increasing his personal fame, than that of the French admiral." Many of his colleagues would readily agree.

Louis-Marie Vicomte de Noailles (day No-Eye) is

one of the most promising of the young noblemen that accompanies d'Estaing to Savannah. De Noailles is brother-in-law to the Marquis de Lafayette, their having married sisters. At the young age of twenty-three, he is commanding a division.

He is handsome, he is athletic and he is known to be one of the best dancers of the day. He is also a proficient musician, being accomplished on the violin. His mother is the celebrated Madame Etiquette, the origin of the term and well-known in French history as the lady-in-waiting to Marie Antoinette.

Equally prominent among d'Estaing's commanders is Arthur Dillon who ranks twelfth in his line of peerage in Ireland. His great grandmother was the daughter of Charles II of France. For generations the Dillons have served the French rulers.

Another of d'Estaing's able commanders is Baron Curt von Stedingk. This handsome Swedish officer is a close friend of Sweden's King Gustave III. Stedinkg will become a favorite of Catherine the Great of Russia in years to come.

Also with d'Estaing, but not as a nobleman, is a youth by the name of Henri Christophe from Grenada. Some say he came to Savannah as a servant to a French officer. Whatever his capacity, he will see the day when he will have a title greater than any of the French nobleman. Christophe will one day revolt against French rule and become King of Haiti and build the mountain citadel of Sans Souci.

Command in the French army and navy usually went to the well known and influential. In observing the French entourage it is not hard to see that behind all the pomp and fleurs-de-lis, the titles and ancient names that the seed of discontent and revolt will soon be planted in France itself.

Way down in the ranks among the French in Savannah are two young soldiers whose futures will be filled with accomplishment and admiration. Both will bloom in the years to come and touch greatness. One is a young corporal named Jean-Baptiste Jourdan and the other is twenty-five year old private Claude Dallemangne. The time is still ahead when both will ably serve Napoleon. Joudan will become Marshall Jourdan and Dallemange will be one of Napoleon's bravest generals.

At the lowest echelon of the French army and navy are the humble enlisted men. Many have been aboard ship since they sailed from the West Indies. For months they have received no pay. Most can neither read nor write. Not that it makes any difference since letters from home never seem to reach them and theirs never reach their homes. Scurvy aboard ship is rampant. The sailors' skin is gray in color and they are often described as having the mark of death on their faces.

For months the American leaders have been asking the French to come to their aid. On many occasions d'Estaing has been told that the American cause is in great peril. One of his fellow countrymen, now serving in the continental Army in Charleston, has especially urged him to come. He emphasized to d'Estaing that in the South, everything is in a state of confusion. He says there are few regular troops in the field, no help coming from the northern colonies, the militia is feeble and poorly disciplined and there is constant friction among the commanders.

Finally, d'Estaing relents and answers the repeated appeals. He knows if the British army in the South is destroyed and Savannah is again in American hands, the British overall strategy for the war will perish before it is born.

Gen. Lincoln, who commands the southern forces, hastily concentrates all his available troops in assisting d'Estaing in a projected attack upon Savannah. Gen. Lincoln and Gov. Rutledge of South Carolina reluctantly admit to the French that their army for the most part is in total disarray. The time of enlistment for many troops has expired and they have returned home. Still, they promise to the French they will field a thousand men by September 11th and they will stand ready to cooperate with the French army.

Savannah Under Siege

The Patriots March

After the battle of Stono Ferry, the American cavalry under Polish Count Pulaski has encamped on a ridge about fifty miles northeast of Augusta. This position actually serves two needs. Provisions are accessible and they are within an easy ride to either Augusta or Charleston if the occasion might require.

Pulaski is a Polish nobleman who fought the Russians then fled Poland when Russia partitioned his homeland in 1772. Benjamin Franklin, in Paris to solicit for the American cause, recruited him. Pulaski has been permitted to form his own cavalry under his command. He is ordered by Gen. Lincoln to join Gen. Lachlan McIntosh, who has recently returned to Georgia, and now occupies Augusta. McIntosh has been in voluntary exile in the North for almost three years following his duel with Button Gwinnett.

McIntosh commands three companies of Georgia militia. Other militia companies were disbanded when the British took Savannah the prior December. With this small command, McIntosh is ordered to move toward Savannah in advance of Lincoln's army that is on its way down from Charleston. He is directed to attack British outposts and open communications with French troops on the coast.

For the combined attack on Savannah, Lincoln orders McIntosh to march his three hundred and fifty militia from Augusta to Ebenezer. McIntosh takes a position outside Savannah between the town and the Ogeechee Ferry. Once d'Estaing makes his landing, McIntosh retires to Millen's Plantation and awaits the arrival of Lincoln. Lincoln hopes that by Sept. 11th he can collect all his available forces at that location. He names McIntosh as his second in command.

The Americans from Charleston are now strung out on the long road to Savannah above Purysburg. Included in the detachment is young Col. John Laurens of Charleston. Laurens is always conspicuous in his regimental uniform and long plumed hat. He is one of the most appealing and dedicated young men in the Revolution. Laurens is the son of Henry Laurens, the close friend and mentor of Gen. McIntosh. Henry Laurens served as a president of the Second continental Congress and is reputed to be one of the richest men in America. The Laurens are devout French Huguenots.

In 1772 at the age of seventeen, John was sent to Europe to complete his education. Ultimately, he studied law in England until his return home in 1777. He joined Washington's staff at the age of twenty-two through the influence of his father. John has an impetuous temperament and from an early age has always been reckless. Washington considered him rash and Gen. Nathanael Greene called him a glory seeker. Quickly, he gained a reputation for taking dangerous risks and courting death. He is said to be charming, radical, generous, candid, bold, warm, a crusader for the equalization of wealth, a stout defender of freedom for black slaves, and a pleader for leniency toward loyalists.

Also with the Carolina detachment is little Francis Marion who would later gain notoriety as the legendary "Swamp Fox"; Sgt. William Jasper, already practically a legend for his many acts of courage as an American scout; and Thomas Heyward, Jr., who signed the Declaration of Independence from South Carolina. Other members include Gen. Isaac Huger, Col. Peter Horry, Dr. David Ramsey, the historian, and the former British major, Pierce Butler, whose father is an Irish peer. Butler's grandson will marry the English actress, Fanny Kemble, author of *Journal of a Residence on a Georgian Plantation,* an expose about slavery in coastal Georgia. It, published at the time of Lincoln's Emancipation Proclamation, along with Harriet

Savannah Under Siege

Beecher Stowe's *Uncle Tom's Cabin,* will do much to stir the growing abolitionist feelings in the next century.

Thomas Pinckney from Charleston is also in the group. He is thirty years old, tall and thin. His hair is dark and wavy and frames his birdlike face. As a member of the landed aristocracy in South Carolina, he and his older brother, Charles Cotesworth Pinckney, have been educated in England. Thomas has acquired a knowledge of Greek and French that enables him to read both languages as easily as other men read their newspapers. Before returning to America, he studied law in London and spent a year at the French royal military academy at Caen.

Lincoln arrives at Zubley's Ferry at Purysburg on the 13th of September. There, he encounters a considerable challenge in getting his army across since the British had destroyed all the available boats when they withdrew. Lincoln orders Col. Laurens to scout the area for rafts and boats. He is concerned that the pontoon boats McIntosh is bringing from Augusta will not arrive in time and further delay his army. Laurens is able to find only two canoes and a rowboat but is able to repair a raft for the crossing. The smaller canoe can only carry three men at a time but the larger one can handle fifteen men and the raft about twenty.

Once across the river, he continues his march and reaches Cherokee Hill, about eight miles west of Savannah. McIntosh joins with Lincoln on September 15th to give a united command. Meanwhile, Gov. Rutledge dispatches boats down from the Carolina coast to assist the French in ferrying soldiers, stores, and cannons ashore.

The American troops are so confident, being allied with the French, that Gen. Moultrie expresses regret that he cannot be in Savannah to share the glory but anticipates with pleasure hearing the joyful news of the surrender.

South Carolina sends six continental regiments, all of which have been decimated as a result of sickness and desertion. Hardly a thousand men are left in the whole lot. Not having been trained in military etiquette they are a slovenly looking group at best. They have unflapped their hats and discarded their leggings. Most are unkempt with uncombed hair and unshaven faces. Appearances aside, their fighting qualities, many times demonstrated in past engagements, more than make up for their dishevelment.

Gen. Pulaski, with his legion, has advanced ahead of McIntosh's force and has already crossed the river into Georgia. He dispatches a message in French to d'Estaing, informing him that Gen. Lincoln, accompanied by artillery and six hundred troops, is close behind. Pulaski estimates the continental forces to be about a thousand troops; eight cannons and two hundred and sixty mounted cavalry.

He adds that Gen. Lachlan McIntosh is also on the march. He is leading the small Georgia continental detachment that is marching down from Augusta. Accompanying him are also three companies of Georgia militia. The names of some of the soldiers in that army would later be prominent as the names of Georgia's counties: McIntosh, Twiggs, Jackson, Baker, Houstoun, Habersham, Meriwether, and White.

Col. Samuel Elbert, captured earlier at the Battle of Briar Creek, had described the continental regiment of Georgia as being a medley of old muskets, rifles and fowling pieces. There are times that all that can be found for wadding for the muskets is dry moss. The appearance of the men is shabby with most of the troops wearing shoes that have been crudely fashioned from animal hides. It is rare to see any two men with uniforms alike. There are cocked hats, beaver hats, round hats, leather hats - even straw hats. Their clothes are a combination of homespun and buckskin. In fact, it looks as though deerskin jackets have become the Georgia uniform.

Before long they will discover they are in sharp contrast indeed to the brightly regaled Frenchmen.

Savannah Under Siege

America's patriots will soon be agog at the parade of French officers resplendent in royal blue coats with scarlet vests and high black boots. Then too, there are the individual French regiments with their identifying colors of green, yellow, violet and black. Only Pulaski's unit, of all the American troops, will be able to impress the French, and they do. Pulaski's hundred lancers (mounted troops) arrive well equipped and their horses are impressive. Pulaski already carries a well-earned reputation for his mounted prowess and is credited with introducing Cossack riding to America.

It is said he can ride at full speed, throw his pistol into the air, catch it as it falls then hurl it to the ground in front of him and leaning over his horse, recover it in full stride without even slowing his speed. Many American cavalry officers have attempted to emulate his feats. Those so foolish have met with predictable results and many have been injured in their attempts.

H. Ronald Freeman

D'Estaing's Demand

When the French fleet is sighted off Tybee Island, Prevost sends word for Col. Maitland to evacuate Beaufort and make haste to Savannah. Shortly after, the French ships disappear and Prevost sends another dispatch. This one countermands his original orders and directs Maitland to stay in Beaufort but on alert and ready to move at a moment's notice. If additional information is gained showing Savannah to be d'Estaing's real objective, Maitland is not to risk being cut off. The couriers bearing these dispatches are intercepted and as a result are unable to get through to Maitland.

Prevost is not aware of the intercepted dispatches and anticipates Maitland's reinforcements. It would have done much to ease his mind had he known that on September 12th, Maitland was pulling out of Beaufort with his nine hundred troops and making for Savannah. With his withdrawal, Britain's only stronghold between New York and Savannah was being evacuated. The detachment is comprised of Scottish Highlanders along with German Hessians.

Since being stationed in the South, Maitland has greatly enhanced his already formidable reputation. In the battle at Stono Ferry, by keeping a cool head, he was able to repel a strong attack by American forces. He repeatedly rallied his troops and made sure they were placed in proper positions. Gen. Prevost arrived with reinforcements as the battle ended and only could applaud Maitland's gallant behavior and prudent tactics.

Maitland's immediate problem now is that the way to Savannah by land is choked off by Lincoln's troops and the route by sea is blockaded by the French. He concludes that the inland water passage, in all probability, will also be sealed tight. Another problem is that almost a hundred of

Savannah Under Siege

Maitland's men are diseased. Many complain that the air of the region is impure and has to be unhealthy. Maitland himself has contracted malaria or what the physicians of the day are calling the "bilious fever".

D'Estaing has chosen Beaulieu, thirteen miles below Savannah, as his primary landing point. Philip Minis of Savannah has recommended this site as the best place for landing and forming up a large number of troops. Col. Joseph Habersham of Savannah meets d'Estaing and his longboats at Ossabaw Island and leads the landing party through the inland waterway to Beaulieu.

D'Estaing feels the spot is poorly chosen since it will only take a few strategically placed troops to pin them down on the bluff and repulse the landing. A military man would have known this. However luck is with them and they encounter no opposition. Fortunately for the French, their only casualties are two soldiers, both wounded when their muskets accidentally discharge as they attempt to scale the steep river bank in the dark.

The first night they spend on American soil is bizarre for the French. It is their first exposure to the eerie Spanish moss combined with the sounds of a summer night in the American South. They have no way of knowing where the enemy lurks and so are unaware that Gen. Prevost has already drawn his outposts back into the city. The French soldiers are tired. Some of the troops have been in open boats for three straight nights.

Locating Beaulieu in the sea of marshy shoreline had been extremely difficult. With all the tidal creeks and islands along the coast, confusion was rampant and delay was frequent. To add to their frustration, the French have brought no tents and the men are totally exposed to the elements. They also have no cooking utensils and when they are able to find a big washpot to make soup, they are all forced to dip and eat from the same cauldron. Hunger prevails over hygiene and they don't seem to mind. The second evening they endure a rain so heavy that it leaves them in a wretched condition. It so totally drenches their firearms and cartridges that it renders the weapons unusable without refurbishing.

The French also dispatch a smaller body of troops ashore at Bonaventure Plantation on the Wilmington River. This is near the settlement of Thunderbolt and only about three miles from the city. Many of these troops come ashore with scurvy and general illness after their stormy crossing from Santa Domingo in Haiti. Even after they land, the wet weather and chilly evenings instill a fever in many of the men. In fact, there are twelve officers and over two hundred soldiers who are unable to make the march to Savannah and must remain at a makeshift hospital at Bonaventure.

D'Estaing dispatches a message to Casimir Pulaski expressing his wish to have Pulaski as the first of the continental officers to join him. Meanwhile Pulaski, from his headquarters at the Habersham Plantation of Silk Hope on the Ogeechee Road, sends a message to Gen. Lincoln saying he intends to meet with d'Estaing as soon as possible.

Pulaski proceeds on to Beaulieu where upon his arrival he and d'Estaing cordially embrace in the rain. It is still four days before Lincoln's arrival. Pulaski has never been able to master English but is fluent in French and quite vocal in that language to d'Estaing with his criticism of the crude Americans.

The French begin to move toward Savannah on the 14th of September and by the 15th, they have joined with the troops at Bonaventure. By the morning of the 16th, the French, two thousand strong, have pillaged themselves to within three miles of the town. They are like a swarm of locusts passing through the countryside. Lincoln's army is at Cherokee Hill west of Savannah on the Augusta Road.

D'Estaing exudes confidence. His primary goal now

is to beat the Americans in what he sees as a race to capture the prize of Savannah. He knows the city will soon fall into his hands and the prize is much greater than Grenada. It will be quite a feather in his cap. As he closes his eyes he can already hear the adulation of the crowds back in France lined up along his parade route.

D'Estaing advances to within a mile of the city with one hundred and fifty of his grenadiers. These are the elite of the French infantry troops that are normally assigned to the front lines. They fulfill this function in all French armies, playing a role similar to the U.S. Marines. His emissary, Capt. Moran of the Dillon Regiment, is sent to Prevost with a summons to surrender. Moran is chosen because of his ability to speak English and to be able to judge the British reaction to d'Estaing's proposal. His uniform is changed from Irish to French and he speaks with no Irish accent at all.

In his most haughty manner, d'Estaing calls for Prevost to capitulate and surrender himself to the arms of his majesty, the King of France. He says he will hold Prevost personally responsible if he attempts a defense that he characterizes as "manifestly vain and ineffective." He also informs him that he will be "nominally and personally answerable henceforward for the burning, previous to or in the hour of attack, of any ships or vessels of war or merchant ships in the Savannah River as well as any powder magazines of the town." He adds as a afterthought to his demand that he has been unable to refuse the army of the United States uniting itself with that of France. A strange thing to say about your allies. Perhaps d'Estaing is only voicing agreement with his press clippings that describes him as the "wonder of the age."

H. Ronald Freeman

The British Fortify

Time has become a precious commodity for the British. From Fort Charlotte (Fort Wayne today) on the eastern end of the city, they can see for miles across the marshes toward the sea. Prevost knows that somewhere out there, Maitland is coming with his men.   So Prevost plays for time. He sends word to d'Estaing that before he can give an answer he must confer with Sir James Wright, the royal governor. Prevost also responds that d'Estaing must know he is a better soldier than to surrender on just a general summons without specific terms. He requests conditions he can honorably accept. D'Estaing refuses terms saying, "terms should be proposed by the besieged and not the besieger." The exchange drags on into the afternoon. Every hour is precious to the British and Prevost is using every ploy possible to give Maitland more time.

Prevost counters the surrender demand and suggests a 24-hour truce. He justifies this action by telling d'Estaing it should give them adequate time to consider the question of surrender. Since there are various interests to consider, he says it is necessary to have time to deliberate. By this time it is nine in the evening. The British have gained a day and during this time they are feverishly entrenching themselves. D'Estaing is aware that this is going on but feels it is of a little importance in the larger scheme of things.

The British only have about twelve hundred troops in the town. These are spread out along a semi-circle a little over two miles along a line that connects the eastern and western ends of the long river bluff. Prevost knows, based on reports from his scouts, that in addition to the French forces, the American troops are again marching on Savannah to join them. He knows too, that as a unified force, they will be too much for him.

Prevost is a soldier whose reputation is one of

personal courage under fire and vast experience. Of course all leaders have their detractors. Many feel he is diffident and possesses no opinion of his own. The British commander Col. Archibald Campbell, who captured the town earlier in the year and has since returned to England said, "Prevost seems to be a worthy man but he is much too old for active service."

Prevost himself expresses the opinion that the campaign necessitates the physical stamina of a younger man. He admits the humid climate and rigors of war have begun to make him feel the effects of his age. Earlier, he had put in a request to be relieved of his command in Georgia. His request was granted and even now, he knows his replacement should be in route. His wife and children have accompanied him from St. Augustine and are present with him in Savannah.

There is much pessimism in the British camp. It is to be expected. They are outmanned and outgunned. Prevost attempts to bolster the morale of the troops by assuring them the enemy are mostly North Carolinians and based on their performance at Briar Creek, they are not expected to be a very determined foe. Everyone in the British camp continues to look toward Beaufort with hope that Col. Maitland will be arriving any day.

The British are also very conscious of the rumors circulating about how the Americans will sack the city once it is recaptured. They know the patriots are eager to make reprisals and retaliate for the harm done to their persons, their families and their properties. The Americans have fresh memories of the British seizure of the town less than a year before. The finest of their furnishings were smashed and left in the mud and grime in the streets. Not only was there looting, but robbery, arson, rape, and even murder. Now momentum has turned and it is the patriots' turn to smell blood.

Since the British took the town the prior October,

very few measures have been taken to strengthen its defenses. Although a few old redoubts (primary fortifications) have been repaired, very few new ones have been erected. But this attitude of superiority and complacency is changing rapidly and being replaced by an extraordinary exertion in this time of crisis that has suddenly turned to peril. The defenders know they must rise to meet the challenge.

The British immediately set to work four to five hundred slaves to bolster the defenses around Savannah. Many of these are on loan from Gov. Wright's eleven plantations. Many of his buildings and much of the equipment on his property have been dismantled and the materials are being used in making platforms for the breastworks.

Several houses near the town, including Josiah Tattnall's Fair Lawn plantation, are burned so as not to give shelter or cover to the approaching enemy. The British are busy throwing up breastworks and mounting guns that are being transferred from the smaller war vessels in the harbor. Over one hundred cannons are landed and placed in position.

The four redoubts in existence when the French arrived are quickly expanded to thirteen. The ten to twenty cannons initially fortifying the town expand to a hundred and twenty-three. The defense works are composed of a string of redoubts between which horseshoe batteries with gun embrasures (angled openings) are erected. In front of the lines is a ditch and in front of that an abatis. The abatis surrounds the entire works of the town with the exception of those on the west.

The batteries number fifteen and they carry a total of eighty guns ranging in size from six to eighteen pounds (weight of the shell). They have been removed from the ships of war and are repositioned near the line with sailors reassigned to man the batteries, especially a large new redoubt on the west side of town that has been dubbed the "Sailors' Battery." The marines have been merged in with the grenadiers of the 60th Regiment. Even the captains and crews from the merchant ships are assigned a post of duty. Also impressed into service are the citizen loyalists left in the town. Many are sent to man the lines.

The British assess every available resource of man and means and engage them into service. The brilliant British engineer, Capt. Moncrief, is overseeing the town's defensive deployment. In the rear of the lines are epaulements (earthworks) and gun pivots. The entire line is fortified in the front by an abatis that is built of cedar and pine.

The walls are made of sand and buttressed by sandbags. In between the redoubts there are sentries posted to render effective communications. A distance from the city walls measuring about a half mile has been burned and laid bare. It is almost impossible for the allies to close in without being observed.

The principal redoubt is in the center of the city's southern line and when the French first approached on September 16th, it was being used as a barracks. Overnight, the barracks disappeared and was replaced by a formidable battery. Next in importance is the Spring Hill Redoubt that commands Yamacraw Creek and the Augusta Road.

The redoubts are constructed with several angles so the attackers can be drawn in between and hit by crossfire. To their front is a rampart with a parapet and a broad ditch in front of that with an outer abatis constructed of spiked trees and a glacis that slopes down to the fighting plane.

The British fleet stationed in Savannah has been drawn back near the city and the battery on Tybee Island has been destroyed to keep it out of allied hands. Since it is anticipated that the French fleet will want to move upriver, the shore markers pointing out the ship's channel are cut down. Floating marker buoys are also removed from the river entrance. These actions and the river's many sandbars thwart d'Estaing's initial plan to take Savannah by river.

When the British overran Savannah the prior December they had the necessary boats and equipment that d'Estaing's assault is lacking. They had galleys and shallow draft boats to carry heavy artillery and most importantly they had experienced pilots. The French are lacking all of these things. It took three weeks on the river for them to do what the British were able to do in three days.

The British ships *Rose* and *Savannah,* as well as four smaller galleys, are sunk at "five fathom hole" about two miles below the town to further impede the channel. Before the vessels are sunk, their sails are stripped and utilized for tents and their cables are cut into small pieces to be used as ammunition for the cannons.

The British are also concerned about their exposure upchannel. To protect in that direction, a line is stretched across the river above the town to prevent fire rafts being made by the Americans from being floated down with the current into the town. It will also block the French vessels that are able to get upriver by sailing above Hutchinson Island in the north channel, then turning and coming down the river.

Savannah Under Siege

Maitland's Determination

All the while, Maitland's little flotilla continues to crawl cautiously in a southward direction, weaving its way among the coastal islands of Carolina and inching its way slowly toward Georgia. Maitland is hoping the way is still open. It will take only one man-of-war at the mouth of Skull Creek, where Prevost's first message was intercepted, to seal it. The Americans and French are aware Maitland will travel through these waters in his attempt to reach Savannah. His troops are aboard the *Vigilante*, a number of galleys, and several other small craft.

Unknown to the Americans, Maitland is still struggling. He transfers his troops to smaller crafts and leaves the *Vigilante* and larger galleys at anchorage at Buck Island near Hilton Head. There, the sickly disembark. The operation has now reached a critical juncture. Maitland is closing in on Savannah. To reach it he will have to cross the Tybee Roads channel at the mouth of the Savannah River. Even from Hilton Head's Callibogue Sound he and his troops can see the topgallant sails of the French frigates. They effectively bar that route.

If the British are to save the southern colonies for the King, Maitland must somehow get his troops across the twenty miles of marsh and swamp that will be their final hurdle in reaching Savannah. And now, even if they can reach the town, Maitland knows he is probably too late. He cannot imagine the French delaying the attack.

As they say, fortune smiles on the bold, and Maitland is certainly no quitter. His troops, by chance, encounter some black fishermen in the marshes near Savannah. In their melodious Gullah dialect, they inform him of an obscure waterway behind Daufuskie Island near Hilton Head. As the tidal creeks snake through the marsh, two critical streams loop within a short distance of each other. Over the years a shallow channel has been effected to connect the two. This passage, "Wall's Cut," can only be crossed at high tide. To Maitland, it is worth the risk because the creek into which it empties runs straight to the Savannah River and above where the French ships are anchored.

His troops plunge ahead, negotiating a passage never attempted by boats their size but only by criminals, runaway slaves or others in desperate straits. By those not there it can only be imagined the degree of mud and marsh they encounter. Finally, their determination wins out and with the help of a high tide and a thick fog, the Cut is negotiated. Now what remains is the difficult stretch of creek between Wall's Cut and the Savannah River.

The men sometimes sink in mud and marsh up to their waists. At times, the boats are literally dragged and pushed along the narrow creek bed by will of brute force. But when all seems in vain, when the mud of the coastal marshes only seems to suction them down, they are suddenly looking out on the unobstructed current of the great Savannah River. Better yet, there is not a French ship in sight, only swarms of sea gulls and other shore birds begging a free morsel from the passing boats. The French ship's captains have been erroneously informed that if they effectively blocked the mouth of the Savannah River, they would also block the route from Beaufort.

Although one of the French captains is ordered to proceed up river with three ships and anchor as close to the city as possible, many difficulties have been encountered. Cannons must be loaded. The channel is narrow. Sandbars are numerous and depth soundings have to be taken almost every foot of the way. The intent of the ship's movement is not to intercept Maitland, but to pursue and destroy the British ships and afterward establish communication with the French land forces.

As it turns out, the only ships Maitland encounters in the river are the British brig *Keppel* and the *Comet,* a small

Savannah Under Siege

galley.   They have been sent down river in hopes of covering his approach. It is about noon on September 16th when the high bluff of the town comes into view. D'Estaing's demand for surrender to Prevost had only been delivered a short time earlier. When the British troops in town learn of Maitland's arrival, they are ecstatic. The first of his troops file up the bluff and are marched off to their posts in the line. The Savannah garrison is now exuberant.

Maitland's troops are still strung out in small boats making their way up the river. Shortly before midnight, Prevost receives a reply from d'Estaing on his request for a truce. He consents but warns that with the sounding of retreat the next day; it will signal the resumption of hostilities.

Why does d'Estaing agree to the truce knowing the British are being reinforced? There are two possibilities for his action. The first is that he has not yet received the message informing him of the arrival of Maitland's troops. Or possibly, he has heard the bad news and is merely trying to save face. The British are totally unconcerned about his reason. They are elated for a truce that will give them time to have all of Maitland's men reach Savannah.

It would seem that d'Estaing has to know. The French had established a post on the river at Brewton Hill on September 16th. At nine in the evening the lookout pens a hasty note conveying the bad news about Maitland's arrival to d'Estaing. "The Americans have reported", he says, "that fourteen boats passed today, each filled with at least twenty-five British troops who reached the town of Savannah safely." D'Estaing decides the news is worth a personal investigation.

On the following morning it is murky when he and Lincoln look on from Brewton Hill as the last of Maitland's troops enter the town. D'Estaing later comments that if this was not bad enough, Gen. Lincoln fell asleep in a chair while they watched. What d'Estaing does not know is that it is not Lincoln's indifference to what is transpiring as much as his habitual napping. He is known to even nap between sentences while he dictates his dispatches.

With Maitland's arrival there is much controversy swirling over the failure to cut off his troops. Gen. Lincoln maintains that the French agreed in the council of war in Charleston that they would block the enemy at Port Royal. Lincoln reminds them that he warned in early September that it would be necessary that the mouth of the Savannah River, the Broad River in Carolina, the Ogeechee River, and the inlet to Sunbury be sealed. If this had been done it would have thrown up an effective barrier between Beaufort and Savannah.

D'Estaing it seems, had given such an order to d'Albert de Rions under the command of Gen. Fontanges, but he was unable to carry it out. The Charleston pilot they hired refused to carry the ship over the bar even though Capt. d'Albert pleaded in vain.

Gen. Prevost remarks by letter to Gen. Clinton that if the French wanted, the British couldn't prevent them from entering the Port Royal River and by so doing cut a division between their little army. The French commanders continue to squabble over who is at fault. Finally, they all agree that they dominate the local waters and if they had deployed themselves in proper fashion, any passage by the British would have been impossible.

It seems they should have known that an officer as resourceful as Maitland would stop at nothing in his attempt to reach Savannah. Blockading Beaufort was the linchpin of the entire campaign. It demanded primary attention. D'Estaing fully realized it. Failing to cut off that garrison is a big mistake for the allies. If Maitland's troops had been isolated and barred from reaching Savannah, the British would have surrendered without a gun being fired. Most British commanders agreed with that statement.

With Maitland's garrison joining as reinforcements

and Cruger's arrival from Sunbury, the British army is near three thousand, two hundred men present and fit for duty. The French estimate of the British army is as high as three thousand, seven hundred. The strength of the allies is estimated at around four thousand, two hundred regulars plus militia. The American strength is composed of about a thousand continental troops and eleven hundred militia. The French forces consist of thirty-three hundred European soldiers, five hundred forty-five black troops from Haiti, and one hundred fifty-six volunteers from the West Indies.

While the allies no doubt outnumber the British, the arrival of reinforcements suppresses any question of surrender. On the afternoon of the 16th, at the British Council of War, it is the unanimous opinion that the town should be defended to the last extremity. The council is only convened for the purpose of making a showing since it is already well known within what the view of the Army is.

As Maitland arrives in Savannah, he is informed that deliberations are underway in the Governor's council chamber. He hurries directly to that building and joins in with the meeting in progress. Maitland has been through too much in the last few days to hold much with a defeatist attitude. As he hears the word "surrender", he immediately approaches the front table with a hasty step. Those present note that despite his haste and determination, it is obvious he is exhausted with fatigue and fever.

Maitland turns to face the group and begins to speak - slowly and deliberately in his Scottish brogue. As usual, he doesn't bite his tongue. "The man who utters a syllable recommending surrender, makes me his decided enemy," says Maitland; "It is necessary that either he or I should fall." He lets his eyes drift around the room from face to face. Eyes droop in turn as his rivets on theirs.

Maitland's determination instills hope and courage to everyone present. "I abhor the word '*capitulation*' he says. "If I survive and go home to Britain, I will report to the King the name of the first officer who dares to propose capitulation." Those in attendance hear him loud and clear.

The truce is near expiration when Prevost delivers his answer to d'Estaing. It is to be ended by the evening gun which is always fired an hour before sunset. Prevost replies, "The unanimous determination has been made that we cannot look upon our post as absolutely inexpugnable, yet that it may be and ought to be defended." He goes on to say, "the King, my master, pays these men to fight, and fight they must, and we decline your terms."

D'Estaing is all alone in negotiating with Prevost. The Americans are still attempting to reach Savannah. The pontoons from Augusta are delayed and have not arrived at Zubley's Ferry. Gen. Lincoln's forces, now combined with McIntosh's, come in on the 16th, the same as Maitland, and camp west of Savannah.

D'Estaing has been lulled into a state of overconfidence by his total lack of opposition. After all, hasn't he landed at Beaulieu without opposition? Hasn't he been able to march his troops to the outskirts of the town totally unopposed? He even records in his journal that he expects the British resistance in Savannah to be very feeble. Actually, he is right and at any moment before the arrival of Maitland, a determined attack would have easily taken the town.

Gen. Lincoln, as co-commander of the allies, was not even given the courtesy or opportunity to review d'Estaing's surrender proposal before it was delivered to Prevost. The Count's position is that it was such a small thing that it was certainly not worth disturbing Lincoln after his long march. Feisty little Francis Marion of South Carolina thinks the quarter given the British is unconscionable. "My God!" he cries, "whoever heard of such a thing before! First allow your enemy time to fortify and then fight him?" Marion knows what havoc the

Savannah Under Siege

Americans at Bunker Hill had been able to wreak on the British when they were given the time to fortify.

Lincoln admonishes d'Estaing for ignoring American interests and d'Estaing tacitly agrees that all future negotiations with Prevost will be conducted jointly by the allies. Privately though, d'Estaing voices his opinion to his close associates. He says Savannah is a British possession and as such, a legitimate prey for French conquest. Also, d'Estaing feels his army is superior to Lincoln's, not only in numbers but in experience and ability as well.

Allies Dig In

The reinforced town makes a frontal attack by the allies, both a doubtful and costly proposition. There are only two other options - leave immediately, which they think to be a bad idea or, lay siege to the town. Because of politics, they elect to stay. If the French depart, the Franco-American alliance is in jeopardy. More importantly, d'Estaing will be under criticism not only in America but also in London and probably even Paris.

There must have been a debate raging in d'Estaing's mind. If he withdraws, many will say he has secret orders not to assist the Americans. It will be a never-ending source of complaints and suspicions between the allies. In his mind he already has one incident hanging over his head. The year before, he sailed away from Newport to engage a British squadron but ran into a storm and sustained severe damage to his vessels. He was unable to resume the operation. Because of this, the siege had to be lifted by the Americans. Commander Nathanael Greene was exasperated. "The devil has got into the fleet," he commented. Others quipped that the French were the "heroes of flight." D'Estaing now can ill afford a charge of deserting his allies a second time.

In order to improve their position, the French move from an initial position southeast of the town to one almost due south. Dillon is in command of the right side, d'Estaing the center and de Noailles the left. The field hospital, the cattle depot and the powder magazine are still farther to Dillon's right. To the left and southwest of the French, Lincoln's troops are bivouacked. They face toward the east with the swamp of Springfield Plantation to their rear. Pulaski's Legion is a little south of the junction of Bull Street with the Ogeechee Road, which today would be the site of Monterey Square.

The French and Americans are camped between

what today is Anderson and 31st Streets and from Waters Road to the Ogeechee Road. The series of French trenches begin at Gwinnett and East Broad and extend to Lincoln and Wayne. There are French batteries at the present day intersection of Waldburg and Abercorn and Waldburg and Lincoln Streets.

On the night of the 22nd, the French dig-in, directly in front of the British center. Less than three hundred yards away from the British fortifications, the French entrench themselves up to their chins. From there, they gradually move to within two hundred yards of the British.

Siege tactics in the eighteenth century consist of digging a trench parallel to the wall under the cover of night at a range of about a thousand yards and mounting a battery. Using this as cover, a communications trench is dug forward in a zigzag manner to avoid direct fire and a second parallel trench and battery is established at about four hundred yards. This battery then covers the digging of the third parallel trench, which is about seventy-five yards from the wall. At this point cannons are fired point blank against the walls to effect a breach. Most fortifications surrender after the third parallel is firmly established. Capture is considered certain if this is successfully completed.

On the other side, the besieged are not totally passive. They can always disrupt the digging with sudden sorties (attacks from the besieged) as well as destroy siegeworks with cannon fire. More often than not what was taught in the military schools of the day was not the art of defending strong places but that of surrendering them honorably after certain conventional formalities. That is why Lincoln and d'Estaing are certain Savannah will fall when the allied force comes before it.

The Savannah siege, however, can only follow the textbook up to a point. It fails because the allies are not positioned to follow eighteenth century siege procedures.

H. Ronald Freeman

The problem is that d'Estaing has not the luxury of time. His fleet is anchored in a most hazardous position on the coast and the West Indies are defenseless as long as he is in Georgia. Crucial to all siege operations is the coordination of the land attack and the sea defense. D'Estaing's problem is the inability of the French fleet to hold indefinitely off the Georgia coast while the land troops complete the job.

Now the hopes of the allies are staked on intimidating the defenders into surrendering and by a bombardment of the town. Delays continued to plague the allies. Siege entrenchments are begun on September 24, but progress is slow.

Cannons and mortars are brought in with great difficulty from the fleet by the way of the new depot established at Thunderbolt on the Wilmington River. This is closer to the town and makes for better logistical support than the Beaulieu base. However, lack of horses and artillery carriages prevents them from landing the heavy artillery, which is not in place until October 3rd.

In addition to the French guns, the Americans are also able to construct a battery and arm it with four six-pound cannons. This is their entire artillery strength but they remain optimistic about their chances and confident the British will capitulate. Lincoln agrees with d'Estaing that it will only take the sound of a few large cannons combined with the first bomb thrown into the city to bring about surrender.

Along with other problems there is the unspoken problem of lack of unity. The allied forces are allies in name only. Especially in the French camp there is no unity, even among the officers. So many noblemen are officers it is difficult to maintain any real discipline.

One of noble birth is inclined to consider himself on the same social level with his fellow aristocrats even when they outrank him. And then, even among the nobility those

Savannah Under Siege

favored members of the court frown upon those whose lineage stems from the provinces and of course, both lord it over the commoners. But even with all this class division, the French seem to maintain an esprit de corps. This is even more amazing when you consider one of noble birth becomes a lieutenant as young as fifteen, whereas the common soldier is fortunate to even reach the grade of petty officer after twenty years of service.

D'Estaing's army is quite a mixed affair. The regulars are drafted from at least fourteen different regiments and his black volunteers have been recruited in the West Indies. As in most armies, the regulars are prejudiced against the militia and do not relish fighting alongside them. There is also prejudice against the free black troops from Santa Domingo. These men have just left a country where racial unrest is being stirred. The French officers know the importance of harmony being maintained.

D'Estaing is always careful to emphasize that the black soldiers are to be treated with the same equal consideration as the whites. Specifically he says, "they aspire to the same honor and will exhibit the same bravery." But among the blacks there are also wide social distinctions. Even among the mulattos there is a pecking order of privilege. The black troops recognize as many as thirteen separate subdivisions among themselves. This only adds to the disunity.

D'Estaing himself is aloof and extremely unpopular with some of his fellow officers. His meteoric rise has incited much jealousy in the navy where he is felt to favor the "blues," who haven't risen through the ranks. D'Estaing's original military service has been in the army and he is still referred to in naval circles with derision as being an infantryman. D'Estaing acknowledges his critics but rebuts that many other French naval heroes have not been promoted through the lower grades. He feels if he is successful in the great things he plans, the glory for him will be even greater if he is saddled with the same disadvantage they had.

His critics are of strong opinion there will be no such glory awaiting d'Estaing. Although he has proved himself formidable on land, it is obvious he is hesitant and overcautious at sea. After the battle for Grenada one of his junior officers stated, "if d'Estaing was as good a sailor as he was brave, he would not have allowed four demasted vessels to escape. Another said, "the opposing admirals are well-matched, Lord Byron of the British is lacking in activity while Count d'Estaing is lacking in judgment."

Even among his own naval commanders the lack of cooperation almost approaches subversion. Apparently a clique has been formed against the Admiral and its members have resolved to thwart and where possible even disgrace their commander. The same thing occurred in Grenada that had been experienced the year before in Newport. When d'Estaing gave the unmistakable signal to put up all sail, several of his captains ignored the order while others in the rear even shortened sail.

D'Estaing features himself an able administrator and does in fact process a vast amount of correspondence and orders. It seems to relax him. Yet most of the time things are in a state of disorganization. A case in point that was almost comical was the situation when the French landed on Tybee Island to capture the little fort at the mouth of the Savannah River.

D'Estaing's reconnaissance reported that it was still occupied by the British. As the Count proceeded toward the fort he looked back and was alarmed to see only a handful of his men following him. He complained to his adjutant general who replied that no orders had been received to bring the troops along. D'Estaing had absentmindedly forgotten his men were still in the landing craft. He neglected to give orders for them to disembark and as a result they passed a miserable night in the boats.

Even so, the situation in the army is not any better than that in the navy. Ammunition for the batteries is scarce and little order exists within the ranks. Wine and spirits are in short supply and American rum is being touted as a substitute. They say the cook shudders along with d'Estaing as he recites the ingredients for this popular American concoction: sugar, water and fermented molasses.

H. Ronald Freeman

Savannah Under Siege

On the morning of September 24th, after a heavy fog lifts, the British light infantry under Maj. Graham makes a sortie with six hundred men against the newly dug trenches. Their intent is only to reconnoiter the strength of the forces that man them. The French however, misinterpret their feint and pursue with bayonets. The French are commanded by Maj. O'Dune who seems to have access to ample stores of spirits and has consumed an excess of wine even at this early hour. His artificial courage and excitement caused by the alcohol carries him beyond the proper limits of pursuit that have been prescribed.

As the French approach the fortifications, British cannons open up and rake them severely. One French officer shouts "forward" as loud as he can while another orders the drummer to beat the retreat. This confusion may be a portent of things to come. In the chaos, three officers are killed and nine wounded, while eighty-five men are officially listed among the dead and wounded. The British sortie is quite a bold move, especially when considering the Savannah garrison is severely outnumbered by the allied forces.

Fortune does smile upon the French the following day when their warships led by the *Sagittaire* captures the British ship *Experiment,* the frigate *Ariel,* two store ships; the M*yrtle* and the *Champion*, the freighter *Victory*, and several small sloops and coastal vessels laden with rice and flour.

The *Experiment* had been demasted in a gale while en route to Savannah from New York making it easy prey for the French vessels off Hilton Head. Her captain, Sir James Wallace, has recently married Royal Gov. Wright's daughter and she is aboard as well. Thomas Pinckney has been assigned to the fleet because of his knowledge of

Savannah Under Siege

French and he has been attached to Count d'Estaing as a liaison officer and translator.

Pinckney knows from Westminster School and goes out of his way to see that as a prisoner Wallace and his wife are treated well. Another passenger aboard the *Experiment* is Gen. George Garth. Garth has been dubbed by the Charleston press as "the hero of Fairfield" after he sacked that New England town. He is on his way to Savannah to relieve Gen. Prevost.

Probably more important to the French than their prisoners is the great quantity of supplies aboard the ships. Twenty-two hundred barrels of flour, oatmeal, beef and pork are seized. In addition, they gain the payroll of thirty thousand pounds sterling destined for the garrison at Savannah.

D'Estaing sends word to Prevost, to let him know his payroll has been captured. The British troops are only paid every eight months and d'Estaing is certain the absence of pay will convince them to surrender. It does not.

Not only do the British not surrender but on the night of the 27th, a small raiding party, under Maj. McArthur, advances toward the Americans for the purpose of destroying both the newly dug trenches and weapons. They approach with stealth and in such a manner that they are undetected and able to lure out troops from both American and French positions. Immediately they withdraw, still undetected in the darkness. The French and Americans, each supposing the other to be the enemy, begin exchanging fire. Losses are sustained in both camps before the error is discovered. Again, as with the aftermath of Maj. Graham's sortie on the 24th, the British look on with amusement.

In addition to the disunity in the French camp, there is also a lack of harmony between the two allied camps. Gen. Lincoln, as mentioned earlier, is totally disturbed that D'Estaing has demanded the British surrender in the name of the King of France. He only learns this after the fact when the Count sends a copy of the correspondence to Lincoln. Nowhere is there a mention of the Continental Congress. D'Estaing's rebuttal was, how could the British surrender to an army that has not yet arrived?

Although the Charleston newspapers may lead one to believe there is constant harmony between the officers and men of both allied armies, obviously, such is not the case. When you look a little deeper you find there is little love lost between the French and the Americans. Mutual esteem and confidence among the allies is at a low ebb. The Americans are held in such low regard by the French that they are not even allowed to venture into their camp. There are certain perimeter lines that American troops are forbidden to cross without a written permit. If for whatever reason they do venture into the French area without a pass, they are promptly arrested.

It is indeed a strange quirk of fate that brings these armies together as brothers in arms. A blending of old France with the rough-hewn backwoodsmen of Carolina and Georgia. Their bond of mutual interest is a slender thread and only a mutual enemy binds France to America. Even so, in the opinion of the French rank-and-file, the Savannah campaign is an ill-conceived enterprise that holds little merit for French involvement.

There continues to be recriminations for failing to prevent Maitland from joining Prevost. D'Estaing, of course, blames Gen. Lincoln, saying he is possessed with a selfish desire to be first in on the capture of Savannah rather than doing his duty and containing the British at Beaufort. He reports to his ministry in France that to cover up their error, the Americans are lashing out with altercations, reproaches and false accusations against the French.

And what about Lincoln?   The French officers generally are not very impressed with the New Englander with the rotund figure commanding the American forces. How can they be? He has no bad habits. He neither curses nor drinks. D'Estaing openly criticizes Lincoln on many occasions and even comments on his lack of opinions. He does not deny that Gen. Lincoln is a brave man. But he does repeatedly berate Lincoln for allowing Maitland and his troops to break through to Savannah. According to d'Estaing, "the Americans continue begging, even demanding our support." This he adds much in the way of explaining why the French stay on after Maitland's arrival.

What kind of person is Lincoln? By most descriptions, he is a patient soul. It is said that his character melds the patient philosopher with that of a pious Christian. These are traits that obviously hold the American commander in sharp contrast to the quick tongue of d'Estaing. The Count is constantly complaining about everything and especially the American food. Obviously, his continental palette is not at all attuned to such delicacies as cornbread and rice cakes.

The Americans, the terrain, the troops or the leaders encountered during the Savannah expedition, do evidently not impress the French. They describe the American Army as being made up of deserters and adventurers from almost every country. Baron Curt von Stedingk, a Swedish officer in the French army, writes that the rebels are "so badly armed, so badly clothed, and so badly commanded, that we can never turn them to much account." On top of all this they do manage to compliment the continental regulars who conduct themselves in a superior manner at all times as compared to the American militia.

D'Estaing, like his officers describes the American generals as being fraught with forgetfulness, deviousness, petty jealousy, and an incredible ignorance of their own country. But surprisingly there is one person in America that d'Estaing really looks up to. When the French fleet was anchored in Boston, John Hancock as President of the Continental Congress presented d'Estaing with a full-length portrait of Gen. George Washington. D'Estaing was ecstatic. His kinsman and fellow countryman, the Marquis de Lafayette, was present at the time and made the observation that he had never seen a man so happy to possess a picture, including that of his sweetheart. The Count hung the portrait in a conspicuous place on the *Languedoc* and wreathed it in laurel.

It is near midnight on the evening of October 3rd when Savannah is awakened by the first barrage from the sixty-seven guns and mortars from the allies. The crash of shells is from the land batteries but when the firing stops and later commences it comes from another direction - the river. This firing is from the French ship *Truite* that is armed with twenty-eight 12 and 18 pounders and is anchored in the Back River off the eastern end of Hutchinson Island just below the city. The *Truite* wanted to go farther up channel but was stopped because of the shallowness of the water.

Going upriver has been extremely slow since they have constantly had to sound fathoms to be sure the depth of the water was adequate in the uncharted river to keep them from running aground. Another impeding factor is they have had to wait for tides and winds to round the many bends and received no help from the experienced pilots in the area. Most of who are loyalists. The *Truite* is built for oceangoing, not river navigation and because of this draws too much water. Because of its extreme distance from the city, the *Truite* inflicts little damage to the town. Suddenly, after about two hours, the firing ceases. What happened?

There are two stories as to why the firing stops so suddenly from the *Truite's* batteries. One is that d'Estaing fears his supply of ammunition will soon be exhausted. The other, and more truthful story, is that the firing is stopped, at the insistence of Col. de Noailles. It seems a

Savannah Under Siege

number of the shells have fallen around the trench he commands. In looking into the matter, the French find something serious but comical. The ship's steward, in error, has supplied the French naval cannoneers with a keg of rum as opposed to their normal ration of beer. By 4:00 a.m. the firing recommences, still with more volume than precision.

On October 4th, fifty-three heavy cannons and fourteen mortars begin a five-day bombardment of the town. The shelling fails to crack the defenses but causes considerable damage within the town. An American officer writes, "The poor women and children have suffered beyond description. A number of them in Savannah have already been put to death by our bombs and cannons." One of Prevost's aides comments, "Many poor creatures are being killed trying to get to their cellars, or hide themselves under the bluff of the Savannah River."

More than a thousand shells fall on Savannah. They shake the ground and explode with great firebursts. The people who can, run to the cellars. It is reported that even there they cannot escape the fury of the bombs. The unofficial count is that forty women and children lose their lives in the bombardment. Many citizens die but only one soldier. Ensign Pollard of the 2nd Battalion of Gen. DeLancey's brigade is killed the first day of shelling.

Loyalist Chief Justice Anthony Stokes describes one night of the shelling and its effects: "At five I am awakened with a very heavy cannonade from a French frigate to the north of the town, and with a bombardment which soon hurries me out of bed; and before I can get my clothes on, an eighteen-pounder enters the house, sticks in the middle partition, and drives the plastering all about. While we are in the cellar, two shells burst not far from the door, and many others fall in the neighborhood all around us. In this situation a number of us continue to stay in a damp cellar, until the cannonade and bombardment almost cease, for the French to cool their artillery; and then we ascend to breakfast."

It is hard to find a house that isn't damaged by the firing and some are totally destroyed. It is actually much safer on the front lines than back in the town. Realizing this, Gov. Wright and Lt. Gov. Graham move to the front and pitch a tent next to Col. Maitland's. Following suit, much of the populace move to the same sector.

The noise of the big guns can be heard as far away as d'Estaing's ships off Tybee Island. In addition to shells, the French hurl cannonball carcasses filled with turpentine that set many buildings on fire. It is the French expectation that the whole town will be in flames but it is to the credit and diligence of the firewatchers that only two houses are burned to the ground during the siege.

The cannonballs just seem to bury themselves in the sand of the town. In spite of this, damage is massive. Few buildings are undamaged. It is said the town is so torn to pieces and subdued that other than shrieks from women and children, little is to be heard. The people who can, huddle in cellars below the river bluff, sharing their quarters with huge wharf rats that are probably more menacing than the cannonballs.

Where possible, mounds of earth are placed around houses and casks of sand are used to strengthen the foundations. Gen. Prevost's wife and children reside in a damp cellar and use their featherbeds to bolster the walls in making it bombproof. Lachlan McIntosh, the American general and Savannah resident, has his wife and five children penned up in the town as well. Many of Savannah's ladies, fearful of staying in the city, present themselves at the French camp for protection.

The siege is not one where either side defers to the comfort and safety of the fairer sex. On the 29th of September, the Americans under a flag of truce request a conference. Maj. John Jones, a planter from Sunbury and aide to Gen. McIntosh, asks that Mrs. McIntosh and her children be permitted to leave the city. Prevost refuses. Maj. Jones comments that it is a pity because Gen. McIntosh's entire family is there.

On the 8th of October, Gen. Prevost proposes to d'Estaing that the noncombatants in town, including his wife and children, be permitted to go down river on a ship until the business is decided. The allies refuse. Many of the town's women and children are sent to Hutchinson Island across the River. It seems that the town's citizens, both white and black from every quarter, flock to the plantation there.

The batteries continue their fire. As time drags on, the residents become complacent about the bombardment. They learn to fear the cannons and mortars less than the telltale sound of small arms fire. Even the children, as initial fears are quelled, learn to dash in the streets and cover the freshly fired cannonballs with sand. When the shells are cool enough, they gather them up, cart them to the British and receive sixpence for each in return. Obviously the British make good use of the shells by hurling them back at the French and Americans in the trenches.

As each day passes, the allies realize the bombardment is nowhere near producing the results they expected. Very little damage is being rained on the British fortifications. The primary French battery is positioned at too far a distance for breaching the walls. When the French are fortunate enough to silence a British cannon, it is quickly replaced by another located even farther to the rear and with better protection.

It seems with all the shelling the small Charleston battery inflicts the worst visible damage to the British fortifications. It is somewhat comical. Their youngest artillery officer asks for and receives permission to fire the first American cannon. The shot goes awry and shears the flagstaff on the British defenses.

The French begin to realize the opportunity they missed by not attacking the first day. Civilian deaths and destruction of property are not the persuaders necessary to achieve the desired purpose of the allies - that of compelling a surrender. Doubt and discouragement begin to creep into the journals and letters of the besiegers. "Any hour, we expect them to capitulate," writes Maj. John Jones on October 7th to Polly, his wife. "However," he adds, "many agree with me they will not - not until we compel them by storm."

Jones joined the militia forces in December 1778 when Prevost first invaded Georgia. The British have confiscated his house, land, slaves and business. He is a devoted Presbyterian who believes in predestination. He feels that every soldier's wife should resign themselves to believe likewise. He writes to Polly, "if it's in my fate to survive this action, I will. If otherwise, the Lord's will be done." He writes again, "as soon as this important affair is over, I shall immediately return home."

The two sides are now at an impasse. The British have been busily strengthening their fortifications daily. The south wall of the barracks has been leveled and the British have reduced their side to a good parapet height from the floor. It has been three weeks since the French commanders decided that storming the British lines would be much too costly. Now that option has become what the Americans refer to as "the forlorn hope."

Savannah Under Siege

The Forlorn Hope

Something must be done. Supplies are scarce and time is running short. The hurricane season is upon them. D'Estaing has already borne witness to the fury of these storms when he engaged the British fleet off Newport. Initially food around Savannah was plentiful and the troops lived on the fat of the land. That has changed over the weeks and now they are even without bread. The only staple available to them is that Georgia dish that most Frenchmen detest - rice.

The allies as besiegers are in a position of want, whereas the British as the besieged have enough provisions and ammunition for an extended resistance. It is an ironic turn of affairs. According to British inventory they have enough flour on hand to supply six thousand men until January 25th; sufficient meat to last until March 25th; and enough rice and oatmeal to supply the town through March 13th. In addition, cattle numbering in the hundreds have been driven into town before the allied entrenchment.

Manning the trenches day and night has virtually worn out the French troops. Violent thunderstorms have added to their misery. They feel they have endured more than ample exposure to the Georgia climate. During the day it subjects them to the most intense heat and at night to bitter cold. The French troops had departed the West Indies unprepared for the change of weather and have brought only their lighter linen uniforms.

Back in the fleet, things are even worse. Bread aboard ship is two years old and so much decayed and worm-eaten and so disagreeable to the taste, even the domestic animals on board refuse to eat it. The ships are being supplied from Charleston but service is extremely slow and in meager amounts. Add to this that the main staple seems to be rice and that requires water and pots for cooking. They don't have either. This renders that staple almost worthless.

Illness is prevalent and there is little medicine. Most sailors have neither coats nor shoes and are almost naked. They have little to eat except salt provisions. This makes them extremely thirsty and there is very little water. In fact, they are down to their last two days of fresh water. Of these sailors, the few who are in condition to work the ships are weak and tinged with a livid color with the mark of death painted on their faces. Sailors are succumbing to malnutrition and disease and are being tossed overboard at the rate of about thirty-five bodies per day. Many of these use their last breath to curse d'Estaing.

D'Estaing has a sadistic sense of humor that seems to surface at the most improper times. For instance, when it is reported the ships are leaking and there is a shortage of drinking water, d'Estaing says in jest, "they complain of having no water yet the ships are sinking because their holds are full of it."

His naval commanders are particularly bitter about conditions aboard ship. They see themselves and their crews as victims of d'Estaing's Georgia campaign. There they are, multiple vessels anchored on an open coast with no harbor. They are also in the hurricane season with precious little in supplies and a shortage of anchors. Several of these have been lost in the storm encountered in their passage from the West Indies. D'Estaing also had forbidden the men upon their leave from the West Indies to take anything more than a canvas coat and two shirts. In addition to being subjected to the elements, the crews are riddled with sickness and have no hope of fresh provisions. As they suffer, they believe the troops in town are living on the fat of the land while they are stuck on the ships.

The Count's original intention was to be in Savannah no more than eight days. He so informed the Americans when he arrived. His army has now been on shore for three weeks. Upon their arrival it was summer but now the geese are beginning to fly south and the nights have become chilly.   Still hanging over their heads is as well is the threat of British pursuit. If Admiral Byron pursues d'Estaing from the West Indies, his undermanned ships will be like so many lame ducks. Even worse, a hurricane could destroy the fleet at any moment.

The fleet is still crippled, mostly in its rigging, from the storm it encountered en route from the West Indies. The ships are short of cables, tackle and anchors. Much of the crew's time has been spent installing temporary rudders. The *Magnifique* is magnificent in name only. She has sprung such a large leak that a merchant vessel is tied against her to maintain her flotation and her pumps are required to be kept going day and night. Her seventy-four guns have been transferred to another vessel that can withstand the weight.   D'Estaing's commanders run the risk of being attacked by the British fleet while their ships are in a weakened condition and with a great many of their officers and men on shore. D'Estaing's officers continually inform him of the dangerous situation the fleet is in. D'Estaing finally acknowledges their petitions knowing the time has come where his position must be assessed.

The British too have commented they don't feel the French can continue in such an exposed situation off the coast at this time of year. The fleet has been in its current location for over a month, a position where the British never dared to remain for more than eight hours, even in beautiful weather.

By now the time has arrived that d'Estaing usually refers to as the"*beau moment*", that is, the point where success is imminent. In Savannah the *"beau moment"* has not arrived and this is no ordinary siege. Even with all the allied effort, nothing has been achieved. New fortifications have arisen within the town while the old are neither abandoned nor taken. Even if the allies capture a position they still face additional entrenchments farther to the rear. d'Estaing comments, "this strange siege is truly a Penelope's Web."

He needs input from his engineers so he will know how close they are to being in position with the final parallel trench of the siege. The engineers' response is what d'Estaing has suspected. Employing the usual siege methods, it will take another ten days to reach the British lines.

Weighing all the inputs, and after much deliberation, d'Estaing decides he must attempt to overcome the enemy with an all-out frontal assault. Actually, d'Estaing never intended to carry the siege to conclusion. He could not afford the hazard to his fleet. He had only hoped, by a protracted siege, to convince the British that it was his intention - and hope for their surrender.

Another obvious alternative is to abort everything, pull out and sail away. That is the logical move but simply out of the question. After all, French honor is at stake. The option of the "forlorn hope" must be chosen after all. The moment has arrived that d'Estaing has described in a letter three weeks before. He said, "after all other resources have failed, one must take sword in hand." It is one of d'Estaing's favored phrases. At heart he is a true grenadier of his Majesty the King. The only question that remains is where to concentrate the attack?

Both sides have their informants and deserters from the British camp have revealed that the western side of the town fortifications facing the American camp is guarded only by militia. D'Estaing too has personally reconnoitered the southwestern corner of the town where the Spring Hill redoubt is located and knows it is the least fortified. It also has the advantage of being able to conceal an allied assault in the woods where they cannot be perceived in advance by the British. At that point, from the woods to the enemy lines, is a distance of about five hundred yards.

Savannah Under Siege

Another advantage to the allies is that the western side has only one trench rather than the two that surround most of the city. D'Estaing further notes the trench overlaps rather than being continuous and that his army can pass between the break. Also the abatis on that side does not extend all the way to the river. Thus it seems to be the preferred location for an attack in force. The disadvantage is that it is too far away for the French batteries to be much help in support. A stream flows from the base of the cliff on which the horseshoe redoubt is built and on down to Musgrove Creek. It is this stream that gives Spring Hill its name.

The Spring Hill redoubt is defended by South Carolina loyalist troops led by Capt. Thomas Tawse and the vindictive Lt. Col. Thomas Brown from Augusta, who once had been tarred and feathered by Georgia rebels. The other redoubts along the western wall are also held by loyalist troops. So the section of the wall that holds the potential for being the bloodiest part of the battle will pit Americans against Americans.

Farther along the western wall near the river, British Gen. Prevost has placed a naval battery of 9-pounders, stripped from the ships. It has been dubbed the "Sailors' Battery." Another naval battery lies to the east of the Spring Hill Redoubt, supported by British marines and grenadiers. This will be used to reinforce the redoubt if the allies attack there.

D'Estaing is not alone in his assessment of the degree of weakness in the western fortifications. The British too recognize the redoubt atop Spring Hill near the Augusta Road as the weakest point in their line. Even Prevost admits the terrain is favorable to the enemy despite all his military engineers have been able to do to strengthen it. There is a marshy hollow west of the highway and that affords the allies an opportunity to approach to within a short distance undetected. About a quarter-mile separates the redoubt from the Sailors' Battery down near the river. Between these two are two more redoubts and a second battery.

The Sailors' Battery is in an advantageous position to strafe the open ground between the marsh and the British defenses where the allied plan calls for the troops to mass for attack. There are also smaller fortifications and outposts that cover the gaps while a strong line of earthworks protect the right side of the Spring Hill redoubt. Another factor in British favor is that the frigate *Germain* has not been dismantled and it is anchored upstream from the town in the river and commands every approach bordering on Musgrove Creek.

From Spring Hill moving due east in a counterclockwise path, there is a redoubt commanded by Col. Cruger and his troops that have been pulled in from Sunbury. They cover the road leading from Savannah to the south. A final redoubt is located on the northeast end of the line, about where Ft. Wayne is today. In command is Maj. James Wright, son of Gov. James Wright.

D'Estaing also notices that the redoubt at Spring Hill is far enough away from the marsh to permit several columns of troops to pass in between and facilitate an attack farther along the British right flank toward the river. His scouts have observed that in the mornings when the animals leave the city to graze between the entrenchments and the marsh they have no ditches to cross. So it is here, at this place, where the allies will strike - with d'Estaing at the head of his troops.

D'Estaing's decision to attack as well as the place of attack brings the usual criticism from his lieutenants. The feedback from his subordinates seems to be a virtual Tower of Babel. Col. de Noailles feels the point of attack is not practicable. Col. von Stedingk feels the difficulty of the terrain more than offsets the perceived weakness in the point of attack. Several others, including Dillon, are in favor of withdrawing. Others maintain it is impossible to a take Savannah with less than five thousand handpicked men. Everyone seems opposed. Everyone of course, except d'Estaing.

The Count, in a predictable reaction, is dictatorial to those who oppose him. He tells de Noailles with disdain that his opinions are those of an old man. The officers present can see the sting of the remark to the young commander. De Noailles pauses only momentarily to conceal his anger and then like a chameleon he shifts into a manner and response that both redeems himself but also finds favor with the Count.

De Noailles is quick to assure d'Estaing that when he goes under enemy fire he will be the young man he is. But, he adds with emphasis, officers of experience are concerned that the place of attack is not the best and agree with his opinion. They think the allied thrust should take place against the south wall where the trenches have been opened.

D'Estaing surveys the room. He then informs his lieutenants in a measured tone that the French have an obligation to the American cause and the honor of the King demands that the siege not be raised without striking a vigorous blow. Thus, the decision has been made. Savannah will be captured and this business finished.

D'Estaing admits that there is a multitude of obstacles but expresses his feelings that extreme bravery will overcome everything. He also believes it is time to prove to the Americans by a brilliant action, although it might be a bloody one, that the French are willing to dare everything for them.

"Everything" is the defining word. They are playing for high stakes indeed. The primary theater of war for British purposes is being shifted into the South. Gen. Clinton's expeditionary force is at this time leaving New York with the idea of taking Charleston. Clinton knows if he loses Savannah he will have little chance of recovering the Province of Georgia, much less overcoming South Carolina. If Georgia is lost; the door could even be opened for American independence. If Savannah falls, Britain's only remaining foothold between Canada and Florida will be New York. The Revolutionary struggle is on the line and Savannah is the arena.

In addition to his other foibles, the Count possesses a strong sense of self-righteousness. He features himself to be a martyr for the American cause. Although he feels abused by the Americans, he says it in no way diminishes his zeal for his allies. His officers look at each other and toward the floor with resignation. They know based on past experience that argument with d'Estaing is futile. D'Estaing stands firm and doesn't capitalize on the input from his brain trust. He does not understand why those surrounding him are not as sold on his plan as he is.

Neither in his capacity as admiral or general, is he accustomed to asking for or accepting, advice. In the opinion of many of his junior officers he is a haughty and vain character. This is the time he needs to listen to counsel but his headstrong nature prevents him from giving an ear to those capable of guiding him, much less following their advice. D'Estaing is a commander who leads by fear. Unfortunately, by so doing, he succeeds only in causing dissension and making himself resented and hated.

What about the Americans? Gen. Lincoln acquiesces and agrees to the plan. He feels it is his only option. D'Estaing is superior to him in rank. Plus, and more importantly, the French are operating as a voluntary force. They have furnished three times as many troops for the joint movement against Savannah as have the Americans. To withdraw, without further effort, would make Lincoln answerable to the taunt of cowardice and the bitter condemnation of all his fellow American patriots. Also, Lincoln had agreed with d'Estaing on the plan in principle.

Much like d'Estaing's officers he is caught up in the torrent and is not in control of the coming surge of events.

Gen. Pulaski too is concerned and presents a written proposal to d'Estaing cautioning against the attack. He feels a better alternative would be three separate points of attack: one on the British right flank along the Augusta Road; another on the British left wing to be made by the Americans under Gen. McIntosh; and the main attack to be launched near the right center of the British line. D'Estaing receives his suggestion only as additional input. The plan has been cast in stone.

D'Estaing feels the redoubts and earthworks on the west side of town can be approached under the cover of darkness with much less probability of detection than either the southern or eastern fronts, thus permitting a surprise attack. The assault is to be a joint effort of French and American troops. The French effort will be two columns consisting of about a thousand men each with a thousand troops held in reserve. The Americans will also furnish two columns, but with both committed to the attacking force.

Optimism is scarce, even in the American camp where they have a greater vested interest in victory. Several of the officers have expressed a foreboding of disaster and have bid their good friends an affectionate farewell. Each is certain he will not survive. Maj. Jones, imbued with his Calvinistic feeling of predestation, feels his time is at hand. Even Count Pulaski has fallen into a state of melancholy. He is unable to find the scapulars that have been blessed by his Church and he considers it to be a bad omen. He is morose and brooding and only the prospect of battle seems to placate him. Still, he tells several of his close friends, he anticipates death in the attack.

Since the decision is final, it only remains how each unit will be deployed. The French will attack the Spring Hill redoubt and against the Ebenezer redoubt to its north. The

Americans will attack the entrenchments between the two and to the north of the Ebenezer Redoubt, which is defended by only seventy-five loyalists. Laurens column is also assigned the capture of the Ebenezer redoubt and the adjoining breastworks.

On the other side, Col. Maitland has been given the both the honor as well as the responsibility of commanding this vulnerable sector. Again, Maitland is dealt the toughest hand. Ninety North Carolina loyalists are stationed with him in this area. These troops are battle seasoned and fully as capable as the British regulars.

Within the French army the two attacking columns will be led by a vanguard of two hundred-fifty grenadiers under Col. de Betisy (Bay-teasy). It consists of three patrols of over sixty men each and its officers are hand picked from two grenadier companies. The vanguard will have the mission of seizing the Spring Hill redoubt while the two main columns pass between the marsh and the redoubt to assail the entrenchments and battery immediately to the north.

The right column will be personally commanded by d'Estaing and Col. Dillon with Maj. Brown as second in command. It will strike at the entrenchments and battery to the left of Spring Hill while the left column under Col. von Stedingk will move on farther north paralleling the wall to the end of the abatis before they turn toward the town.

Col. de Noailles will be in charge of the reserves but under Gen. Lincoln as senior officer and will take no active part in the engagement. De Noailles is to locate and occupy a prominent point where he can observe everything that will transpire. In the event of allied success he will advance to a suitable point and in the case of a reverse, cover the retreat. He will be supported by field artillery close by.

The three columns will further divide into three battalions within each column. Their orders are to form up so they will present themselves to the enemy as three distinct heads of attack.

The American Light Infantry together with the Charleston militia, commanded by Col. Laurens, will comprise the first American column. Lauren's column will be immediately followed by a second American column consisting of the First and Fifth South Carolina regiments under Gen. McIntosh. Laurens will follow the French left column under Col. von Stedingk. The cavalry under Pulaski will attempt to reach the Yamacraw settlement by penetrating the lines between the battery and the redoubt near the river.

The overall assault will be initiated by false attacks by the French at the center and by the Americans on the eastside of the town. An amphibious assault will also be made from the Savannah River. The attack will begin no later than four a.m. on the morning of Saturday, October 9th. Success depends on timing, coordination, and above all - surprise. Of the three elements, d'Estaing emphasizes surprise as paramount. Everything depends on it.

In the words of Robert Burns, the Scottish poet, "the best laid schemes o' mice an' men, gang aft agley." Surprise is not to be. It is not in the cards. A British spy is lurking outside the tent where the attack plans are being formulated. The man is later identified as Sgt. Major James Curry, a clerk from the volunteer Charleston grenadiers. This Judas heads straight to Gen. Prevost's headquarters. His revelation proves invaluable. Although Prevost already knows the attack is coming, he is uncertain of its primary thrust. His belief to this point has been that the French will attack on the eastside of town and the Americans on the west.

During the night while the French and Americans are readying their gear and weapons, the British are busily redeploying their forces. They divert troops to strengthen the positions to be attacked and prepare for a desperate defense of their western lines. Knowing where the main blow is destined to fall, Prevost places Maitland, unquestionably his best officer, in command of that section. Under him are stationed many of the elite troops, men of proven fighting ability who can be relied on to stiffen and continue to resist no matter how overpowering the attacking force against them.

Capt. Tawes is directly assigned the command of Spring Hill while Col. Maitland commands the entire western British line. Connecting the redoubts and extending north toward the river are dirt entrenchments giving ample protection to the infantry and defended by cannons at regular intervals. At the river lies the British frigate *Germain* and two galleys with their guns trained along the front of the western line. At the foot of these defenses lies a deep ditch and beyond it an abitis composed of tree trunks with sharpened branches to entangle the allies attempting to force their way through. Between the abitis and the woods lies a low swampy field nearly five hundred yards wide.

Although Prevost has forewarning of the primary point of attack, he has to protect his southern line as well. It extends almost a mile long. Overall he must carefully allocate his twenty-five hundred troops against an assaulting force of over six thousand. He places only four hundred on the west, a reflection of the confidence he felt in Maitland. Of the four hundred and seventeen men assigned to Maitland, fully half are loyalists from the Carolinas and Georgia. There is a special bitterness between them and the assaulting American patriots. Although there are military rivalries going back centuries between the French and British, they still respect each other as soldiers. Their sentiments are far different from those that govern the Tories and the patriots. Between these two there exists an undying hatred. This no doubt extends from the atrocities each has enacted on the other as neighbors.

There will be little rest for the allies on this night before the attack. The troops are out of their tents at midnight preparing their gear for this coming battle of nations and races. With the British are Scotch Highlanders, Tories from the Carolinas, Georgia, New York and New Jersey, Hessian mercenaries from Germany, armed slaves, and Cherokee and Creek Indians, all serving under a Swiss born general. With the allies on the attack are French regulars and militia, American patriots, Polish hussars, Irishmen serving under the French Bourbon banner, and black troops from the French West Indies.

For identification, Gen. Lincoln instructs his men to place a white paper on their hats to distinguish them from the enemy in the pre-dawn fighting. Each American soldier is issued forty rounds of cartridges and a spare flint.

Earlier that morning, French Maj. Pierre L'Enfant leads a patrol of five men, despite the fire from British lines, in an attempt to blast out the wood at the abitis. Because of green wood and a damp morning, the explosion for the powder at the base of the abitis along with the bold undertaking fails.

So much begins to go wrong for the allies that many in their ranks feel there is an evil star behind the thick, gray fog that hangs heavy in the early morning. The French troops are understandably grumbling. Many of their regulars are being transferred into militia companies. Last-minute changes are being made. Dillon's regiment is split, with three hundred of his men being transferred to Col. von Stedingk. Many of the men find themselves being led by officers new and unknown to them. When d'Estaing receives the complaints from his officers, the Count replies he wants it that way. Again he terminates his opposition. The men know from experience there is no recourse.

H. Ronald Freeman

October 9th

The entire French army takes up arms at midnight and at three a.m. marches toward Lincoln's camp on their left. The French arrive late in the American camp where the attack is to originate. For the most part, they are forced to wait for their guides who prove their undoing. Before the attack, the commanders think they know the direction to march in. But when it's time to go, they lose their way and the troops have no idea where their guides are leading them. Dillon's column misses the proper path and slithers slowly through the adjacent swamps. The delay costs them even more of the protective pre-dawn. This debacle with the guides is typical of the disorganization and lack of planning that marks the onset of the attack.

At the head of von Stedingk's column is posted sixty volunteers elected from all the corps. Guiding them is a Frenchman from Savannah named Roman who is an officer in the American artillery. He is charged with conducting the column on a proper path. Roman has assured the allies that he was part of the building of the defenses of Savannah and is acquainted with all its environs. However, he is referring to the fortifications that had been constructed by the Americans before the attack by Campbell in the prior year. For some time after the capture, the British have not significantly altered the existing works. He is under the mistaken impression it is still the same.

Three redoubts located triangularly fortify the western side of the town. British sailors from the warships and other transports on the river are manning many of the batteries. As they emerge from the woods, Col. von Stedingk asks Roman how far the distance is from his point of attack to the redoubt. Roman answers that the fortifications have been altered and he is unfamiliar with the terrain. He then refuses to accept the responsibility and washes his hands of the entire matter. In Col. Dillon's column the guide chosen is no better. He admits at the outset he is not familiar with the road and then disappears at the first musket shot.

The guides are one problem, pecking order among the French is another. Between their regiments, military etiquette of the day gives precedence in the order of battle according to seniority. Even within the regiment, positions of honor go to companies according to the commission dates of their captains. When the French muster for battle, if an officer is entitled to a more privileged station than that in which he is placed, it is his due to march his company down the entire formation to its rightful place in the order of assault. All this accompanied of course, with drums and fifes playing.

Even in Grenada, a few weeks earlier, d'Estaing witnessed the same sort of behavior in the fleet. Rather than following his signals as to combat formation, the captains put on sail in their race for positions in the battle line they deemed the proper due for their station of rank. This is the way the Bourbons waged war in the time before Napoleon and in the process, lost an empire.

An eerie skirl of Highland bagpipes from the wall pierces the pre-dawn stillness. The sound is not new to the allies. They have heard it many times in the weeks prior. But now the French hear a different melody, the *"Lugubre Harmonie"* a French tune. It emanates from the area of intended attack. This is far to the right of the place where the 71st Highlander Regiment is usually stationed. Usually they are defending the redoubt on the left flank by the Sea Island Road on the way to the Tattnall plantation of Fair Lawn. No doubt the bagpipes make an impression of dread as their mournful sound cascades down on the French troops. To d'Estaing's keen ear, it not only shows that the enemy is aware of his strategy, but that they want the allies to know Maitland and its best troops are waiting.

D'Estaing knows militarily, it is time to abort. But he also knows he cannot. He is a slave at that moment to American opinion and knows that withdrawal will make him an object of derision. In his mind it is better to die, than be laughed at in the Court of Versailles.

The columns march in their divisions with an easy gait so they will arrive at the point of attack on the designated hour. At four a.m. the two allied armies set out together for the Spring Hill Redoubt a mile away. About five in the morning they converge in a clearing about a hundred and sixty yards from the edge of the woods. They are still about a half-mile from the enemy. Here the columns are halted and wait to close up the ranks as stipulated in their orders. The troops grow restless as dawn begins to break. The columns begin to form into platoons for the attack.

The plan is first to march to the left paralleling the wall and filling the ample space between the redoubt and the marsh and especially avoid mixing up the columns by marching too closely together. Then, having spread out, advance to the right and attack the enemy.

Huger's troops that are to attack on the eastside of town are located with his 1st Division at what will become the intersection of East Broad and Charlton, and his 2nd Division at what will become McAllister and Perry Streets, in the angle between Wheaton Street and President Street.

Huger marches to the right of enemy lines and stays as near as he can without being discovered. It is 4:00 a.m., the time the troops in the center trenches are to begin their attack. He advances his troops and tries to attack the wall as near the river as practicable. Although it is intended as merely a feint, if he gets an opportunity he is ordered to capitalize on it and push into the town. After wading half a mile through the rice fields that border the city on the east, Huger reaches his point of attack. As he makes the assault, he discovers the enemy is already on the alert.

Savannah Under Siege

The British troops are under the command of Col. Cruger and Maj. Wright.

Huger had not conducted an adequate reconnaissance and his five hundred troops become bogged down in flooded rice fields from an incoming tide. When they finally do reach the dry ground the British easily disperse them with artillery, concentrated musket fire and even blaring music. His attack retires even faster than they went in and in the process sustains twenty-eight dead and wounded.

The feint in the center by West Indies volunteers and French Marines is also a disaster and meets with considerable loss. They advance from their trenches to the front of the British fortifications and discharge their muskets. Immediately they are met with a return volley and must retreat quickly back to their own defenses. The attack on the center is repulsed by troops under the command of Lt. Col. Hamilton of the North Carolina regiment of loyalists. All in all the false attacks by the allies are not given the slightest attention by the British.

On the west side of town shots are heard from these false attacks. It is the agreed upon signal for the main assault to begin. It is now 5:30 a.m. The allies hear to their right the beginning of a very lively fire of musketry and cannons.

The fog begins to lift and the British sentinels soon discover the presence of allied forces. D'Estaing feels he can no longer wait for the columns to tighten up and assemble. Much of the main force is still back in the swamp not having reached the clearing. He feels he must attack now with the troops that are ready.

The beat to charge is given to the drummers. Suddenly, they are commanded to march forward and the vanguard moves somewhat to the right to take a position opposite the principal angle of the redoubt. D'Estaing and Dillon follow the vanguard and head with the right column straight to the front. Von Stedingk's column moves to the left.

D'Estaing orders an advance at the double quick. He is at the head of the first column. The drums begin to beat the *"pas de charge"* and the columns dash forward. The Bourbon battle cry begins to resound in the damp morning mist. *Vive le Roi! Vive le Roi!* (Long live the King). The plan calls for hacking through the abatis, charging through the ditch and clamoring up the redoubt. The plan is simple and comprehensive but a forewarned enemy is waiting in readiness.

As they move forward, they encounter a hailstorm of fire from the front and both flanks. British soldiers wear white cockades on their hats and white shirts over their coats, imitating the French uniform, to confuse the allies. This shows they are forewarned of the place of primary attack.

The abatis is easily hacked through with axes and as they break into the clear the vanguard embarks into a pell-mell charge through the mire and up to the redoubt. *"Vive le Roi! Vive le Roi!"* Immediately, they are within pistol range of the enemy but a single volley of musketry from the walls and one round of cannon fire cause massive disorder. The vanguard seeks cover in the ditch but finds there is little shielding to be had there. British batteries strafing the ditch take a frightful toll. The vanguard charges a second time, again with no success. A blistering British fire retards the attack.

The right column moves on to attack the stretch of entrenchments to the north. Von Stedingk's left column moves across the Augusta Road and heads farther north to assault the redoubt and entrenchments being defended by Maitland and his Highlanders. The third column under Col. de Noailles remains in reserve and goes to a small elevation about 300 yards to the rear of the field near the Jewish cemetery. From there he is able to observe all movements and immediately move to any point that demands his presence. Several 4-pounders are placed in strategic positions alongside the reserves.

The French right column under Col. Dillon prepares itself to go into action or at least the head of the column does. Many are still back in the swamp and haven't caught up with the leaders. Dillon offers a hundred guineas to the first man who breaks through the hail of fire from the British entrenchments to plant a fascine (bundle of rods) in the ditch below the works. Not a man moves. Mortified, Dillon begins to accuse them of cowardice. After all, his brigade has earned the reputation of "The Wild Geese."

His Sgt. Major steps forward. He says, "Sir, had you not tempted them with money, these grenadiers to a man would have volunteered." Hearing this, all the soldiers advance toward the wall of the town. One hundred ninety-four go forward, but only ninety will return. The column, moving to the left while traversing the marsh, swamp, and brambles, loses its formation and can no longer preserve any order. Many of the troops lose their shoes to the suction of the mud. Many others will lose much more.

The firing is forceful, and although the column is seriously crippled, it crosses the Augusta Road and advances on the right where the attack is ordered. Now enemy fire is murderous as the grenadiers of old France clamor over the abatis. They swarm ahead in their white uniforms like shadows emerging from the mist and storm up the glacis (mound) in front of the Spring Hill redoubt. British muskets cannot prevent the vanguard from advancing toward the redoubt, and the right column upon the entrenchments.

It is here where nearly all the volunteers making up the column are killed. The second in command, Maj. Thomas Brown, is actually entering the redoubt when he is mortally wounded. Dillon and eighty grenadiers reach the entrenchments. It's a bold move that could carry the day if reinforcements come forward. They look back in desperation for assistance but the column is too strung out. The needed reinforcements are not there and when the British appear in force, the French are driven back. Those who overran the trench are not supported and practically all are killed.

Neither the French nor the British have time to reload their muskets. After an initial discharge they rush at each other with bayonets and rifle butts. Hand-to-hand fighting along the entrenchments is desperate. French banners are planted on the berm. British Lt. Thomas Tawes falls defending the parapet, his sword still penetrating the body of a French soldier. He is actually the third to fall to his blade during the morning assault. The remainder of Dillon's column is in total disarray back in the swamp. The assault by the French troops was so eager and this having combined with the difficulties of the terrain has not permitted the French to preserve their ranks and soon they are scattered asunder. Disorder begins to prevail.

The southwestern British line is only defended by a few troops from the 60th regiment, North and South Carolina loyalists, marines, sailors, a handful of dismounted cavalry - a total of only 417 men. The French vanguard scrambles through the ditch which is nine feet deep and up the steep sides of the redoubt and a few even penetrate the defense.

Without reinforcements, the French are gradually driven back as more British troops come up and fan out along the redoubt. Col. Betisy, commanding the vanguard, is wounded in the hand as well as the stomach. They retreat to the left to escape the annihilating fire but quickly become mixed with d'Estaing and Dillon's right column. The attack waves of the French are like those crashing against a seawall and upon being repelled, collide with those behind them that are still cascading forward from the sea.

The retreat is murderous. British artillerymen, their guns almost touching the retreating troops, fire a parting salvo.

The head of the right column has penetrated within the entrenchments north of the Spring Hill redoubt, but having marched too quickly, it's not supported by the rest of the column. Once there, they are shot down and repulsed while the main body behind them also meets with destructive fire from long-range cannons and musketry and is thrown into disorder. Hand to hand combat quickly ensues.   D'Estaing is almost within the redoubt when he is struck by a musket ball. He is pulled away from the British entrenchments and lies wounded among the dead. Removing him from the field is no easy feat. The first men to come to his aid pay for it with their lives.

The vanguard and the French right column have drifted too far to the left. After being violently repulsed, the initial wave must fall back. In doing so they suffer many casualties from the British battery on the right firing into their flank. But overall the retreat is in good order and the French are able to carry many of their wounded with them.

At this moment everything is in such disorder that the formations can no longer be preserved. The Augusta Road acts as a magnet drawing many allied soldiers who are attempting to disengage from the marsh and swamp. The road is totally choked up with men in disorder. The allies are crowded together with barely enough room to maneuver. They are totally disoriented.

Seeing this, the British mount two eighteen pounders on field carriages and place them at the head of the road. From there, they lay down a slaughtering fire with canister and grapeshot; both fired for effect at short range. Canister is a metal cylinder loaded with musket balls that erupts when it leaves the muzzle of the cannon. Grapeshot is somewhat larger, about an inch in diameter. The shot is bound in a canvas bag then tied with cord in a web pattern to give it more manageability when it is loaded. The bag takes on the appearance of a cluster of grapes and hence the name - grapeshot. Both scatter when they are fired and are devastating up to several hundred yards.

Two British galleys, the *Comet* and the *Thunder,* along with the frigate *Germain,* are in the Savannah River, twenty-five hundred feet away, at the mouth of Yamacraw Creek. From there they are sweeping the road with broadsides. The barrage from the ships combines with the constant firing from the redoubts and batteries that are loaded with grapeshot and have homed in on the road. Added to this is the musket fire from the entrenchments, which is concentrated on the spot in the swamps where many allies are up to their knees in muck. The troops fall like wheat before the scythe. A high tide is scheduled for 8:00 a.m. and the marsh is filling up. Nothing human can stand before the terrible cannonade from the British lines.

Chopped up cables from the ships scuttled in the river, chains, nails, knife and scissors blades, bolts and metal scrap of all kinds as well as canister are fired from cannons at short-range. The air is filled with metal cruelly screaming through allied flesh. The only befitting words to describe it are carnage - carnage - carnage. The French, in their white uniforms, are accommodating targets for the sharpshooters on the entrenchments.

Striving for order out of chaos, French officers struggle to reform this huddled mob that refuses to retreat. To their credit, the soldiers strive to regain their ranks. Front ranks are re-established but almost all in the rear remain in a confused jumble. The troops are intermingled and are only able to rally as a mass rather than attempting to regroup.

Scarcely have they begun to do this when d'Estaing orders the drummer to beat the charge again. When the attack orders are given, the troops are not led by the individual officers they are accustomed to obeying. As a result, they pay little attention to anyone. After the first assault is repelled, the allies regroup and launch subsequent attacks from the south. D'Estaing continues to personally direct the assault even though he is wounded in his right arm. Still, he is in perfect self-possession as he stands on the road near the redoubt with his arm in a sling.

Three separate times he rallies his troops and three times sends them forward *en masse* to the entrenchments. The British stronghold just cannot be carried. The duration of the third charge is extended and the British cannons again extract heavy losses.

Despite all the exhortations, entreaties, and even threats from the French officers, the vanguard and right column are invariably drawn to the left and into the marsh. More than half of these troops succumb to the fire or remain stuck fast in the mud. The bravest of troops, the most disciplined of soldiers and even the stoutest of hearts quail as the angel of death spreads his wings over the blood-covered plain. In desperation, an attempt is made to penetrate through the swamp to the enemy's right.

Even though they have express orders to avoid the swamp, a segment of Col. von Stedingk's column makes a circuit to the left. The troops immediately sink to their knees in the bog. The column has lost its formation while pushing forward through swampy ground but has managed to cross the Augusta Road heading north. It receives British fire as it advances through the marsh to attack Maitland's redoubt. It is here that nearly all of the sixty volunteers are killed and von Stedingk is wounded. The column becomes dysfunctional and is raked with heavy fire.

Somehow, even without formation and order, many of the men retreat to the Augusta Road. It seems to draw most of the allied troops. There, they run head-on into the retreating right column of Dillon that has been thrown back. That column and the demoralized vanguard under Col. Betisy, all retreating to the left, collide with those on the road and soon utter confusion prevails again. The road is strangled with soldiers retreating from the swamp on both sides.

A part of the left column under Col. von Stedingk does finally reach the entrenchments beyond the Spring Hill redoubt. Von Stedingk personally plants a flag. He knows they have succeeded and his lingering doubts of failure vanish. Von Stedingk says, "we are resolved to conquer - the whole army with one accord. We crossed the marsh and sunk to our waists. The day must be ours." And if von Stedingk's penetration is sustained, it will be. However, the rest of his column, much like Dillon's before him, is pinned down in the quagmire of the swamp.

As he reaches the redoubt, crossfire cuts his troops to pieces. Even as von Stedingk gains the parapet, Maitland's discerning eye is alert to the menace. The British and French troops clash head on in savage bayonet fighting that spreads along the parapet. Savannah's sandy soil runs crimson with some of the best blood of Europe.

For a moment the sheer fury and determination of the French attack nearly overwhelms the defenders. The French succeed in raising their flag over the parapet. As fighting rages for control, Maitland commits his reserves. British marines and grenadiers launch a devastating bayonet charge that drives the attackers back from the ramparts and into the ditch below.

French assault troops, helpless and exposed to deadly musket and artillery crossfire, are butchered in the ditch. "The moment of retreat," von Stedingk later writes, "with the cries of our dying comrades piercing my heart was the bitterest of my life." A British officer also later described the scene: "Their assault was as furious as I've ever seen; the ditch is choke full of their dead."

Savannah Under Siege

Glory at a Price

Always impatient for action, Pulaski waits for the signal to join in the assault. It is intended that his horsemen shall penetrate the works to the north of the Spring Hill redoubt and pass on toward Yamacraw, capturing British troops as they go. He is to charge in and swing to the rear of the British creating a diversion that will permit the French columns to reform and resume the assault. It's a daring plan but Gen. Lincoln approves knowing the continental troops are heavily engaged. Although the American continentals have been repeatedly repulsed with severe losses, they return again and again, demonstrating their valor under fire.

Pulaski halts his cavalry at the edge of the woods. He, like the others, is aware of the inability of the French columns to penetrate British defenses and that the attack is faltering. Something must be done to rally the troops.

Blue coated horsemen emerge from the edge of the woods and boot their mounts to form a battle line two ranks deep. The squadron wheels left, pauses a moment, and trots out over the open plain toward the enemy. Col. Daniel Horry is in command of the Georgia cavalry with the South Carolina horsemen falling in behind. The dry rasp of steel is heard as Horry's dragoons draw their sabers. Horses and men tense in anticipation as they await the next command.

Pulaski implores the almighty for help and then shouts to his men - "Forwaaard!" With a sharp, clear blast of the legion's brass trumpet, Pulaski's gallant legionnaires break into a brisk canter. And then at his signal, they are off. Two hundred strong riding at full speed behind the Count. The sound is deafening as the earth reverberates under the hooves of their chargers.

Pulaski spurs his black war-horse and rides hard toward the scene of the carnage. Accompanying him is his friend Capt. Bentalou. The Count rides toward an opening in the enemy works. He is determined to lead his legion and a small detachment of Georgia cavalry and charge on through. If the day can be saved, he knows they must do it.

Bodies are pressed forward, legs thrust back, toes down in the stirrups, and lances are tucked tightly under their right arms. Magnificent on his black charger, Pulaski races with sword in hand across the bullet torn battlefield and straight into the British line of fire. For the first minute or so all goes well and the men speed like knights into the fires of hell. Through the fog and smoke from the cannons Pulaski catches a brief glimpse of the Spring Hill redoubt, the impregnable obstacle d'Estaing was to open for him.

As the distance shortens and the abitis looms before the riders, Pulaski confirms that the French have failed. Then, just as they pass the gap between the two batteries, a splattering rain of murderous crossfire confuses the ranks. The British raise their guns and send a blinding hailstorm of grapeshot and canister into the flying formation. Heavy iron balls and lengths of chain plow up splinters of earth and tear gaping holes that ravage the ranks. Wounded horses rear and plunge, throwing their riders to the ground. Still, those mounted go on with crimson banners streaming, trampling over hideous piles of corpses.

The men are stopped at the abitis, attempting to force their way through and presenting choice targets as the British level their guns with the same effect that has marked their fire on the massed French. A few horsemen still charge with velocity and wheel around the edge of the abitis where they are mercilessly shot to pieces by the fusillade of well-aimed muskets. Brave men are struck down and die without a chance to defend themselves at the base of the shell swept redoubt.

As Pulaski approaches the parapet he is well in advance of his troops, hoping they will follow him through the lines if the passage is opened. Carrying the banner of his legion with his left hand and his sword raised high in his right, Pulaski urges his men onward. Then suddenly, without warning and with his horse in midstride, it happens. Pulaski is struck by a shot that throws him from his mount and pitches him to the ground. He has been ripped by a ball of grapeshot that lodges deep in his thigh.

His men look on in disbelief. It can't be - but it is. There is Pulaski, lying prostrate on the ground. Several of his men including Maj. Rogowski turn their horses toward him, thinking his wound is minor. Then they see the gaping wound visible near his right thigh. Also, there is blood spewing from his chest. They dismount and attempt to raise him. Pulaski looks at Rogowski and speaks in a fading voice, "Jesus! Maria! Joseph!" He is a devout Catholic who throughout his life has never wavered in his faith or his devotion to its service. His is a high standard of moral purity as well as patriotism.

Count Casimir Pulaski, descended from Polish royalty, has received his mortal wound. As the shock wears off his men, his second in command, Col. Horry asks for instructions. Pulaski answers, "follow my lancers." His dominant thought is still forcing an opening and seeking to rescue the situation no matter how irretrievably hopeless.

Capt. Bentalou seizes the fallen banner in his right hand, his left having been shattered by a musket ball. He spurs the legionnaires forward a slight distance more until the whole of the already faltering mass recoils from a murderous hail of iron. Their horses winded, their sabers and lances useless, the cavalry spins about and begins flowing between the abitis back again through the grim gap of death. Many legionnaires hold wounded comrades in the saddle as they slowly trail back to their lines.

Maj. Rogowski too, as he kneels by Pulaski, is grazed with a musket ball to the head that slams him to the ground. It renders him momentarily senseless. The lancers are so mauled by enemy fire they also incline off to the left where they are joined by the other cavalry. With Pulaski on the ground the charge is at an end and his legion is intermingled with the column of French troops, which by this time is in full retreat. Pulaski is later removed from the field by Capt. Thomas Glascock of his legion. He has returned through a storm of shot and shell to rescue his wounded leader.

European is not the only blood spilled. Laurens' column follows Pulaski's Lancers and the cavalry of Georgia and South Carolina under Col. Horry. His column is comprised of the 2nd South Carolina Continental Regiment and the First Battalion of Charleston Militia. They are to join in on the attack on Maitland's redoubt and entrenchments but always keeping to the left of the French troops and in the event the redoubt is taken, they will assault the works between that redoubt and the river.

They are instructed to follow the von Stedingk's column until the edge of the woods is reached where they are to break off and take their positions. Laurens' column encounters the same savage artillery and rifle fire that has been raking the French but they fight valiantly on. The column will enter the redoubt on the left of Spring Hill by ladders if possible and if not, by entrance into it. It is expressly forbidden for the troops to fire a single gun before the redoubts are carried.

The American column advances in good order to its point of attack but at the first volley of musket fire, many of the militia break and run. Only about three hundred of the continental regulars remain. Although repulsed with severe losses they return again and again to the assault. They advance to the entrenchments around the Spring Hill redoubt but are unable to scale the parapet in the face of heavy enemy fire. As they huddle in the ditch, unable to advance or fall back, they are slaughtered by the British. Many that are coming up rapidly in their rear tumble into the ditch among the heaps of dead and dying. They are packed in so closely they can scarcely raise an arm.

Part of the 2nd Continental Regiment has become mired in the marsh. Laurens himself becomes separated from part of his command when they are split by Pulaski's lancers and other cavalry retreating to the left. These continental troops will later receive high praise from the French for their courage in remaining in their position, exposed to enemy fire.

There is nothing but death that awaits the American flag bearers who charge the British lines like Tennyson's immortal "Six Hundred" into the jaws of death. Human flesh, no matter how courageous, cannot withstand the rain of death spewed forth from cannons and musket. They reach the slopes of the redoubt but their surge balks and cannot carry. The dead and dying fall into the ditch by the score.

Two Lieutenants, James Gray and Alexander Hume, fall in succession with mortal wounds while carrying one of two regimental flags sewn by Mrs. Barnard Elliott of Charleston. Theirs is of blue silk while the other is of red. Lt. Hume was to have been married the following week. He was a talented artist and had drawn a likeness of his fiancée that he wore tied around his neck. Sgt. McDonald seizes the flag and finally plants it on the berm in front of British entrenchments. The parapet beyond is too high to scale under such a withering fire. The high water mark has been reached when for only the briefest of moments; the regimental colors of South Carolina are brandished in the face of British loyalists of their own state.

As the retreat sounds, McDonald removes the flag and manages to bear it away. Lt. Bush, bearing the other flag, the red standard, is mortally wounded but still able to pass the flag to Sgt. William Jasper. Jasper is forced to hand it back almost immediately when he himself is struck by a musket ball in the lung. Jasper has vowed to Mrs. Elliott that he would never surrender the colors except with his life. Bush is unable to pass the flag again and it falls under him as he topples in the ditch below the British works.

Jasper is carried from the redoubt to the rear by his comrades where he lingers on edge for a brief hour or two. He says with dying breath, "I have the wound that will give me my furlough." He died as he lived, without fear and without reproach. He asked that the sword given him by Gov. John Rutledge for his heroism at Sullivan's Island be given to his father. He said, "please tell him I wore it with honor."

The second American column under McIntosh is made up of his Georgia continentals and the First and Fifth South Carolina Regiments of militia. They are assigned to move the attack farther north and penetrate the British lines close to the river. These lines are defended by a small redoubt and batteries but protected also by the guns of the British vessels in the river.

Gen. McIntosh arrives at the Augusta Road with fresh troops in his column. The scene is one of chaos and confusion that even on the battlefield is seldom equaled. D'Estaing is now a pathetic spectacle standing in the center of the road. He has collected a few men about him including his drummer. McIntosh asks d'Estaing, through Thomas Pinckney his translator, what orders he has for the fresh American troops. The Count, with an absent stare, instructs him only to bear farther left so as not to interfere with the French troops he is attempting to rally.

McIntosh leads his column toward the river and attacks the defenses to the north of the Maitland redoubt. He overcomes the abitis and the ditch but becomes mired in the bog and lost in the fog and is subjected to constant fire from the entrenchments as well as the galleys in the river. He is forced to fall back. In retreat they are struck in the flank with a counterattack by British troops under Maj. Glasier of the 60th Regiment of grenadiers and reserve

Savannah Under Siege

marines. They are pursued as far as the abitis.

The smoke of muskets and cannons hangs tellingly over the scene, gathering denseness and darkness from every discharge. The roar of artillery and the rattling of small arms combine with the faint sound of the bugle and steady drumbeat. These, along with the cries of the wounded all blend in a horrifying cacophony to create the deadly din so familiar to scarred veterans on the field of battle.

H. Ronald Freeman

Retreat

Slowly, ever so slowly - the allies are driven back. As they retreat they can hear the cries of their dying and wounded comrades. By this time many of the militia have taken to their heels. It seems they took flight in every direction even from the beginning of the attack. Baron von Stedingk's column bears the brunt of the casualties. He led nine hundred troops into action and four hundred and thirty-nine officers and men are left behind either dead or wounded. Von Stedingk himself suffers a bad contusion on his leg.

The allies are bold, valiant and persevering but are still rebuffed and slaughtered. For almost an hour they stand gallant before the cannonade that strikes down rank after rank and spreads death by its sweeping furor into every column. At last, seeing further attempt as no more than a useless sacrifice of life, a dejected d'Estaing orders a retreat and the remains of his gallant army are withdrawn from the field.

It is merely an hour after the initial charge, but it is over. The bugle sounds the order to retreat and most of the troops fall back to the south side of the Augusta Road. Even in retreat they are exposed to the concentrated fire from the entrenchments that continually increases in fervor. The fire of musketry and grapeshot is now focussed on the troops retreating through the swamp. At this point the swamps, which were intended as only as the approach, have become the battleground.

About four hundred survivors under Baron von Stedingk retreat without further loss by following the Augusta Road and circling around the swamp. It proves to be a long but life saving detour. The allies slowly reassemble in small groups of stragglers. Many men have been lost in the swamp and not ten soldiers from the same company return together.

Savannah Under Siege

Hearing the bugle signal retreat for the allies, Maitland orders a counterattack. At this juncture the British show themselves openly upon the parapets and fire with their muskets almost touching the backs of allied troops. During the waning moments of the battle, while attempting to unravel this tangled mass, d'Estaing is hit again. This time it's in the calf of his right leg. He is carried off the field and behind the protective crypts at the Jewish cemetery to escape further injury. This is where Col. de Noailles has been waiting with the reserves.

The British vault out of their works in pursuit. But the French reserves under de Noailles stand fast. De Noailles is collected and places his reserves to the utmost advantage. He ascends a small rise in the ground in advance of his troops, so he can see all movements. As he does, his adjutant Calignon is mortally wounded at his side.

As he witnesses the disorder into which the allies have been thrown, de Noailles orders his reserves up to attack the enemy. When he hears the retreat sound, he and his men advance, in silence and in slow step, and in perfect order. He positions his troops in the path of the allied retreat and stands ready to penetrate within the entrenchments in the event the enemy leaves them. He is prepared to cut them off if they do so.

He suffers some losses from long range fire but averts the attempted British sortie that would have proved calamitous and possibly caused the total destruction of the allied forces. The fact that the British decided against counterattack is attributed to the excellent deployment of reserve forces and this prompt maneuver on the part of de Noailles.

De Noailles gives the opportunity for the repulsed troops to reform in his rear. Seeing this, the British dare not venture beyond their lines. De Noailles' quick response prevents the counterattack that could destroy the allied army.   Behind his reserves, the fragments of the two repulsed columns hastily reform themselves and began to march back to the south of the town. By 8:00 a.m. they are again in the camp they had left only a few hours before. Earlier they had envisaged a complete surprise victory and the capture of the town before the sun had risen.   De Noailles constitutes the rear guard and retires slowly and in perfect order.

Savannah Under Siege

Aftermath

As a fresh breeze lifts the fog on this warm October morning, the sun reveals the terrible spectacle of war. An aide to Gen. Prevost says, "such a sight I've never seen before". The ditch in front of the British fortification is filled with the dead, the dying and the wounded. Many of the bodies even dangle from the abatis. French admiral de Grasse says, "a man has to see it to be able to believe it. In describing only the half of it we would be called the utmost exaggerators."

Full daylight now reveals dead and dying French and American soldiers for fifty yards in front of the ditch, many of them impaled on the abatis. Mangled victims of grapeshot litter the field for a hundred yards beyond. Looking over the sight, John Laurens throws down his sword in disgust.

Literally hundreds lie dead in the space of only a few hundred yards. Hundreds more are wounded and crying out. In only an hour, the defender's ditch has been filled with allied dead and farther out, the plain is strewn with mangled bodies. At 10:00 a.m. a flag of truce is sent in by the French to secure a cease-fire for the burial of their dead and the retrieval of their wounded. It is agreed to until three in the afternoon and later, prolonged until dark.

The battle is undoubtedly one of the bloodiest of the American Revolution. It is exceeded only by the battle of Bunker Hill in the number of casualties sustained on a single side. Even the aftermath of the battle presents problems. A lack of linen prevents the wounds of many men from being treated or dressed. There is also a scarcity of surgeons. The doctors know they must prioritize and only attempt to save the less seriously wounded.

The cries and groans of those down rise in a volume of agony, which is shocking, even to those hardened by many a bloody campaign. The British assist by burying the

H. Ronald Freeman

American and French dead who lie where they fell between the abitis and the breastworks. Those who survive their wounds are taken to waiting ships. The French bound to the West Indies and from there to France and the Americans to Charleston. Other less wounded Americans are carried with Lincoln's forces as they retreat back across the river and into Carolina.

The battlefield extends little more than 300 yards from just south of what will become Liberty Street to Oglethorpe Avenue on the north. Within a single hour and within a few hundred square yards there have fallen more dead and wounded than on any other battlefield in the struggle for American independence. Seldom has an army suffered such a massive loss in such a brief period of time.

While estimates of French losses vary, the official summary signed by French officers lists eleven officers killed and thirty-five wounded while there are one hundred and forty of the rank-and-file killed and three hundred and thirty-five wounded - a total of five hundred and twenty-one casualties. American losses are two hundred and thirty-one including both regulars and militia. On the British side only eighteen are killed and thirty-nine wounded.

The amphibious assault from Savannah River never even got started. The two continental galleys chosen to participate met with misfortune. One lost her anchor as soon as they were underway and the other suddenly filled with water. Many believed the ship had been scuttled.

On high ground, west of Springfield Plantation, a trench is dug, deep and long. After stripping the dead of their useful garments, their bodies are placed in the pit. Included are scores of American continentals and militia, French and Irish, all whose lives have been sacrificed.

Pulaski is borne from the field by John Bee Holmes of Charleston and carried back to camp on a litter. It is believed the grapeshot that downed him was fired from one of the British galleys in the river. Back in camp, Dr. James

Lynah extracts the iron ball. Pulaski bears the ordeal with what Lynah calls unbelievable fortitude.

Afterward, Pulaski chooses to spend his recuperation time with the French. He is concerned, probably rightfully so, that while he is confined to the litter, he can be captured and ultimately turned over to the enemies of Poland, the Russians. With his past history, this is a fate the hero abhors. Pulaski is taken to Greenwich (Grin-itch) Plantation on the Wilmington River and placed aboard the American brigantine "Wasp." Several days pass before it sails. Pulaski dies as a result of gangrene from his wound.

There has been much controversy over Pulaski's death and burial. Based on extensive recent research it is believed that he died at Greenwich Plantation on the Wilmington River and was buried at night near the house. Quite a few years had passed when a skeleton, believed to be his, was exhumed. It was reinterred under the handsome monument in Monterey Square in Savannah erected to the memory of Gen. Pulaski. According to another story, Pulaski died from gangrene while onboard ship en route to Charleston and his body was consigned to the depths off the shores of Tybee Island.

The British governor, James Wright, declared Friday the twenty-ninth of October, a day of public and general thanksgiving in Savannah. He observed that the deliverance and preservation of the town and garrison from the formidable combined forces of French and rebel enemies that came against it, was an act of divine Providence and therefore worthy of public acknowledgement. For everyone this was not the case.

The widow of Maj. John Jones, aide to Gen. McIntosh, is reading his letter from a few days earlier. He said, "we have the prayers of the Church and I hope from the justice of our cause that God will decide in our favor." For Mrs. Jones prayer was disappointing. She admonished her husband during the siege that he should know that he has two dear children and a wife whose happiness is very much tied to him. She pleads with heaven to keep him safe and let her have the happy sight of him once more. On the morning of the attack, he tells several friends he expects to die. Like many others, his fears were realized.

Little did Polly know that as she read the letter her husband's body was being discarded without ceremony into a burial trench. The grave is so shallow that he is recognized by a wound in his hand protruding from the earth. His body is removed by a friend so his shattered remains will receive a decent burial. Jones has been practically cut in two by a four-pound shot at point blank range near the Spring Hill battery. Jones Street in Savannah will be named in his honor.

The Georgians who fled the town almost a year before had gathered near Lincoln's headquarters to wait for the surrender of the city. They were eager to return to their homes and plantations. After the shattering defeat of the allies, they are obliged to again seek refuge among those in outlying areas kind enough to take them in.

Savannah Under Siege

Allied Withdrawal

After the battle, the wounded d'Estaing, running a high fever and refusing to be carried, rides on horseback to the French field hospital in Thunderbolt. Accompanying him is Maj. Gen. Francois Vicomte de Fontanges, his chief of staff. De Fontanges has also received a gunshot wound through his thigh. Once there, d'Estaing refuses to speak to anyone and only tells his surgeon, " I have a deep wound, which is not in your power to cure." The general then points to his heart.

His losses have been far too great, and for the second time he has been thwarted while trying to help America's land forces. He sends word to Gen. Lincoln in the afternoon that the siege is being immediately lifted by the French. The logistics of disengagement are turned over to Dillon and de Noailles. The British are accommodative and even loan a few carriages to convey the wounded to the ships.

The French are unprepared for defeat and many of the wounded must be loaded onto their ships that have no food or water to offer them or even linen with which to dress their wounds. Drinking water is being procured from the river at low tide, even as brackish as it is. The French were planning to be drinking and replenishing their supplies from the wells in the city, once they overcame the British.

A few miles away from Thunderbolt, but still on the Wilmington River, another hospital is set up at Greenwich Plantation. It is direly needed since the hospital in Thunderbolt is overflowing and there are still over three hundred wounded men to be cared for. D'Estaing too, finds himself a patient at Greenwich. During his convalescence, his mind keeps drifting back to the days when he first arrived in American waters. He remembers the words of the Marquis de Lafayette, his kinsman and fellow Frenchman, "you are the man I wish to see at the head of the squadron, and the man who pleases my heart."

Lafayette was only nineteen when he came to the aid of the colonists. He was so interested in America's cause that he left his wife and young baby to come. Gen. Washington and Congress scarcely knew what to do with the red-haired, blue-eyed rich teenager from France. Lafayette was a member of one of the richest families in France. Suddenly he just appeared; expecting to be made an officer in the Revolutionary Army.

Later, when France suffers its own revolution, Lafayette sends George Washington the key to the Bastille, the infamous prison the people had stormed. Even today it still hangs in the hall of Washington's home at Mt. Vernon. Lafayette was imprisoned by the French during the reign of terror. His wife's family was among those executed. His wife Adrienne, who was only sixteen when they married, was spared only because Robespierre, her accuser, died before she was executed. In Georgia, Fayette County and the towns of Lafayette and Fayetteville are named in the Marquis' honor. LaGrange, in Georgia, is named for his farm in France.

It seemed that everything d'Estaing attempted went wrong. Everywhere he traveled he seemed to be a little too late. And now instead of bringing back a triumph from Savannah, he will only return home with one more disappointment. He blames his defeat on the Americans and lashes out. He feels because of them, Maitland was allowed to slip into Savannah through the waterways. In his view the Americans have misrepresented everything from the condition of Savannah's defenses to the size and quality of their army. He is also convinced that an American traitor exposed his plan of attack.

The Americans do not deem themselves defeated and implore d'Estaing to stay on. The repulse at the wall did not dispirit their men and they are convinced it was only a mistake in the choice of terrain. They feel the taking of

Savannah Under Siege

Savannah is not in doubt but only suspended because it is not worth the lives that would have to be sacrificed by more rapid assaults.

D'Estaing will not relent. The siege is raised immediately. Lincoln too, implores d'Estaing to stay. He is convinced that if he will, nothing can stand in the way of their success. Even Gov. Rutledge of South Carolina writes to him pleading that he not dash all American hopes by withdrawing when they are so close to victory.

Rutledge finally accepts d'Estaing decision and sends a delegation to see him, suggesting the French retreat through South Carolina and embark the troops from Charleston. However, d'Estaing's mind is closed. The French have had enough. He will embark from Thunderbolt. The bloody reversal at the Spring Hill redoubt has been d'Estaing's way of discharging the pledge that France has made to support America.

Both Dillon and de Noailles protest and argue the advantage of Charleston as the base of retreat. As an object lesson, d'Estaing sends word that he wishes the retreat to be effected where he has decided and if his two young colonels persist in their opposition, he will appoint Bougainville to command the army. D'Estaing emphasizes what they already know, that it was a compliment to them that he did not appoint Bougainville in the first place. Not only did Bougainville's rank entitle him to the command but he is also an excellent officer.

D'Estaing relents somewhat and does permit part of the embarkation to be made from Causton Bluff, a short distance north of Thunderbolt. It is on the same river and probably a more protected anchorage than Thunderbolt. D'Estaing fears if he retreats to Charleston, his troops will desert by the hundreds in order to find homes for themselves in America. Sentinels are already being placed around the French camp to prevent desertions. American recruiting officers will have an abundant harvest with the

Dillon Regiment thought d'Estaing. It is filled with Irishman.

* * * * * * * * *

The allies depart in separate directions; the Americans leaving a day before d'Estaing's troops start their embarkation. The French are totally unmolested by the British who seem content enough by the fact the French are leaving. In d'Estaing own words," our troops have returned aboard the vessels not only without leaving anything behind but even more than that, without having been attacked, annoyed or even followed."

There are some that suspect collusion between the French and British officers. Young French officers visit the town daily, a fact that is bound to generate suspicion. Even in the town there are puzzled faces. British loyalists themselves think it very extraordinary that their troops never attempted to harass the French in their retreat.

Finger pointing between the allies soon sets in. A French naval lieutenant describes the Savannah operation as an "ill-conceived enterprise without anything in it for France," while a young French artillery officer blames the patriots for the defeat at the Spring Hill redoubt. The "rout began with the rebels," he wrote, "they took flight first...like a crowd leaving church." D'Estaing blames Lincoln, saying the rebels "promised much and delivered little."

General Lincoln speaks not a word of criticism about the French. In his opinion, the cause of failure was the uncertain events that happen in war and are rather to be lamented than investigated. In his usual gracious manner Lincoln writes an appreciative letter to Congress about d'Estaing. "Although he has not succeeded according to his wishes and those of America, we regard with approbation his intentions to serve us, and that his want of success will not lessen our idea of his merit."

For d'Estaing monetarily, things were not altogether bad. The ships captured at Savannah brought a high degree of prize money. Also he received an offer, from the

Savannah Under Siege

President of the Supreme Executive Council of the State of Georgia, for a grant of twenty thousand acres of land and the right of American citizenship.

D'Estaing does in fact receive the land grant in 1784, five years after the battle, at which time the privileges of citizenship are also conferred. At that time he confides to his friend, Thomas Jefferson, that the status of being an American citizen is very dear to his heart. He also felt it was his due since he was the only French general who has shed blood for America as he later boasted to George Washington.

H. Ronald Freeman

Assessment

There is no question that America owes d'Estaing a great debt. In a critical time, he responded. With no prevailing orders from his King, he brought an army to Georgia to mount a campaign that could have turned the whole course of the revolution. His own blood was shed as well as that of many brave Frenchman in the attempt to take Savannah. While it is true that mistakes were made they should not be laid entirely at his door. If, on October 9, 1779, fortune had smiled on d'Estaing and the French, his name would be as familiar in America today as Lafayette's.

When the news of the British victory reaches London, the Park and Tower guns are fired, an act reserved for only great occasions. In classic British understatement, Gen. Prevost informs the high command that "we got both the French and the Americans off our hands, in a manner which we humbly hope our gracious sovereign will not think unhandsome." The British will henceforth always refer to the battle as " the ever famous Ninth of October" or "the Glorious Ninth".

The failure of the assault by French and American forces upon British lines affects the entire course of the Revolutionary War. After this battle, British Gov. Wright of Georgia said, "if the province had fallen, America would have been lost. Gen. Prevost's troops have preserved the Empire." The defeat of the allies at Savannah is celebrated not only in London but also in New York with parades. If Georgia had been lost; the only foothold in America remaining to King George III would have been the city of New York. The defeat of the allies in Savannah gives British morale a tremendous boost and steels Britain in its decision to subdue America.

If Gen. Clinton did not hold Savannah, it would have been necessary for him to totally rethink his timetable.

Savannah Under Siege

There is no question that had he lost Savannah it would have prevented his moving ahead with the projected attack on Charleston. Savannah was the key to enabling the British to mass a large-scale operation against the Carolinas. The British victory at Savannah allowed them to proceed with their new strategy for America, the crushing of the southern colonies, one by one. It was a cruel blow to French pride and to American hopes.

The defeat for the Americans means they are in a worse position in the South than they were before the French arrived. The British can now run expanded operations south of Savannah. The American Revolution is about to begin one of its bloodiest phases. If the allies had retaken Savannah, all the bloodshed and excesses of the revolution in Georgia and the Carolinas for the next three years could have been averted.

The failure to oust the British from Georgia is disastrous for the America's quest for liberty. The war had been stalemated in the North and had the British lost their foothold in the South, it would have shortened the war immeasurably. Historians will say that an allied victory in Savannah would have inflicted a near mortal wound to the British and saved not only oceans of blood but also much of the barbarous warfare that followed in the Carolinas.

The siege in Savannah pointed out the major weakness in the American military efforts during the revolution. The cause was being fought by a hundred heroic armies rather than by one effective, central force.

D'Estaing, in planning the assault, should have known that by attacking with a single column before the rest of the armies closed up and reached their positions, doomed the army to be beaten in piecemeal. What happened is that rather than the British being assailed on different parts of their front, they found themselves only attacked at one point at a time. Therefore, they could concentrate their total fire on a single column. This was repeated time after time with only a different column brought forward for the attack.

D'Estaing also should not have left the French islands in West Indies exposed without protection. This afforded the British a three-month opportunity to retake St. Vincent's or even Grenada. Also, if he had remained in the islands, he would have benefited from an excellent winter harbor. He left Martinique exposed. She was already enfeebled by having her troops continually withdrawn to participate in expeditions like Savannah.

After the victory at Grenada, why did he wish to pursue a far off victory in Georgia rather than returning to France in obedience to orders from the court? He left Count de Grasse in the West Indies with only eight vessels to protect them. The answer probably lies in his being excited by his recent success and seduced by the possibility of further glory. It led him to believe the conquest of Savannah would be an easy matter and consequently one he was unable to resist. He needed new triumphs to add to those he had already been able to achieve.

Savannah Under Siege

Epilogue

After debarking Georgia, d'Estaing's once great armada was buffeted by a severe gale. The *Languedoc*, his flagship, snapped a mast cable. The other cable had to be cut and the big vessel was forced to sail eastward. It was one of seventy French ships that lost its way off the Savannah coast. The *Languedoc* had also lost its anchor and was prevented from returning to anchorage by contrary winds. Its sudden departure left several of d'Estaing's captains on the Georgia coast without specific orders. After repairs, d'Estaing set sail for France, still unsure of his reception.

Once back in his home country, d'Estaing asked the King through an emissary that he be allowed to fall at his feet in appreciation for the confidence he had shown in him. The King replied to the envoy, "absolutely not, it is in my arms that I will receive him." As it turned out, the French people remembered the victory at Grenada and not the defeat at Savannah. Versailles followed suit.

The people gave d'Estaing a hero's welcome. Hobbling around on his crutches, he knelt before the King who expressed extreme satisfaction with his conduct. As his carriage passed through the countryside, flowers were strewn before it on the road. A massive crowd waited for him at Versailles, following him to the house of ministers. There was an air of triumph everywhere. It was not to last.

Before too long d'Estaing was caught up in the maelstrom of the coming French Revolution. He saw the unrest and attempted to warn the monarchy of the coming danger. He even wrote an eloquent letter to Marie Antoinette, the Queen, in 1789 alerting her to the danger ahead for the royal family. Unfortunately his advice was neither solicited nor followed. He incurred her lasting displeasure when as the commander of the French National Guard he didn't turn his guns on the people. She felt a "whiff of grapeshot" fired upon the people could have ended the revolution before it started. That failing, there would be six blood-filled years until a young French officer by the name of Bonaparte arrived on the scene.

D'Estaing continued to steer a devious and dangerous course in the swirl of French politics. When he testified at the trial of Marie Antoinette he said nothing that would implicate the widow of Louis XVI. But it was futile. His testimony not only was unable to free Mademoiselle Antoinette but it worked to his own detriment. After her trial, his house was searched and although no incriminating papers were found, several miniatures of the King and Queen were confiscated. These were considered counter revolutionary propaganda and d'Estaing was brought to trial in 1794.

D'Estaing is remembered as saying, "when you cut off my head, send it to the English, they will pay you well for it." The Count kept his appointment with the guillotine on April 28, 1794. He was sixty-four years old.

Col. Dillon had confided to Col. von Stedingk while in Savannah that he had a premonition he would die a violent death. Like his commander d'Estaing, his appointment came also during the French Revolution. He was guillotined in 1794 and died gallantly. As he reached the scaffold, a lady about to be executed said, "do you wish to go first?" He doffed his hat to her as he ascended the platform and said, "what I would not do for a lady." As he went to his death he shouted the French battle cry, *"Vive le Roi!"*

De Noailles became the leader of the liberal element among the French nobility. He warmly endorsed popular reform during the early stages of the revolution. But as the revolution accelerated, he eventually had to immigrate to America. He chose Philadelphia and was able to add to the already considerable fortune he brought with him. Back in France, during one bloody month in 1794, the guillotine ended the lives of his wife, his grandmother and both of his elderly parents.

De Noailles had been prominent at Yorktown as one of the negotiators of the peace treaty. He re-entered the French military in 1803 and was soon stationed in Santo Domingo in the West Indies. This time, the roles were reversed from what he had in Savannah. Now, de Noailles was the besieged and the British were the attackers. He was finally able to escape the British after being under siege for several months.

His ship was flagged down by a British vessel whose captain inquired if he knew the whereabouts of Gen. de Noailles. In flawless English, he replied that he too was looking for the general. That evening, his ship eased alongside the unsuspecting British corvette. De Noailles personally led twenty grenadiers as they leaped from one ship to the other. A fierce battle in the dark ensued and de Noailles received a serious wound. The French were victorious and the British vessel was captured but de Noailles died a few days later in Cuba.

Sweden and France both honored Col. von Stedingk for his bravery in action in Savannah. He returned to Sweden in 1783 and was eventually promoted to the rank of major general. In 1790 he went to St. Petersburg and soon became the most influential representative at the Russian court. Von Stedingk was one of the great men in Swedish history of the day. A soldier and diplomat of unusual ability.

The patriots in Savannah were so thoroughly overwhelmed by the disastrous failure of allied forces to capture the town that they were brought to the very verge of despair. After the departure of the French and the retreat of Lincoln, Savannah and coastal Georgia reached a pitiful low. Pillage and inhumanity reigned. There were plundering bandits roving unrestrained and actively seizing livestock, furniture, wearing apparel and anything else they desired. Children were severely beaten to make them tell where their parents had hidden their valuables, personal property or money.

South Georgia still remained under the British heel and was forced to pay the penalty of its unsuccessful rebellion. Now there was added resentment from the British because of the recent attempt by the patriots to expel from their borders the civil and military representatives of the King.

Licentious language and lewd conduct of the British soldiers made a residence in Savannah, especially for the ladies and those not aligned with the British crown, almost unendurable.

Agriculture and commercial ventures were totally interrupted. Inflation was rampant with sixteen hundred dollars in paper money equal to only one dollar in gold. On top of all this, smallpox raised its head. Fortunately, inoculation and severe measures succeeded in restoring health to the unhappy community.

Gov. Wright required all citizens to give a very detailed account of their conduct during the siege. He and the military authorities promised protection to all patriot sympathizers who would lay down their arms and submit peacefully to the restoration of English rule.

Organized resistance was out of the question. The patriots were too small in number and too enfeebled by the fortunes of war to undertake the recapture of Savannah. There were a number pining away in captivity and others combating hunger and striving to acquire food and replenish their barns for their families. There were active groups of patriots defending the frontier not only from the torch and scalping knife of the Indians but also the inhuman depredations and outrages of their loyalist neighbors. Still others were following the flag of the continental army and doing battle within the confines of sister states.

Savannah Under Siege

Finally with the recapture of Augusta by the patriots in June 1781, the control of upper Georgia passed into their hands. Lt. Col. James Jackson was ordered to move in the direction of Savannah and occupy positions as near the enemy as caution would allow. Generally, his instructions were to annoy the British outposts and detachments as completely as the means of his command would allow. In January 1782, Gen. Nathanael Greene ordered Gen. "Mad Anthony" Wayne to march toward Savannah in an attempt to retake that city. Wayne was instructed to keep a close watch upon the enemy and if the opportunity arose, attempt the recapture of Savannah by a nighttime operation. At that time about thirteen hundred British troops and about five hundred loyalist militia occupied Savannah. As Wayne slowly encircled, the British forces withdrew into the still fortified town.

As the two sides faced each other, Gov. Wright was officially notified of the proceedings of Parliament recognizing the independence of the United Colonies. This in turn was communicated to Gen. Wayne with a proposal for a cessation in hostilities. Wayne agreed and offered citizenship to the British loyalists who were interested. Those unwilling to convert went with their families and personal property to Cockspur and Tybee Islands. There, they awaited transport ships to take them back to England.

On July 11, 1782, British troops evacuated Savannah and in the afternoon Gen. Wayne entered with his forces and took possession of the town. Lt. Col. Jackson, in consideration for his meritorious service in the advance, received the keys to the town as a token of formal surrender. He enjoyed the pleasure and honor of being the first to enter Savannah from which the patriots had been forcibly expelled in December 1778.

So three and a half years after the capital of Georgia was wrenched from the patriots by royal forces it was restored to the Sons of Liberty. Independence became a reality but it had been won at great cost.

And what happened to the American participants? Many went on to greatness and their names have been memorialized throughout the region. Thomas Pinckney became governor of South Carolina, congressman, and Minister to Great Britain. His brother, Charles Cotesworth Pinckney, also became a diplomat and was twice the unsuccessful Federalist candidate for president. William Few, Pierce Butler and James Jackson would go on to be U.S. Senators. Jackson also served as governor of Georgia and in congress. Pierce Butler and William Few were members of the federal constitutional convention. Joseph Habersham of Savannah was Postmaster General under Presidents Washington, Adams, and Jefferson.

Many counties bear the names of the men who fought on the American side in Savannah. Sgt. Jasper was honored not only in Georgia but in South Carolina, Mississippi, Texas, Missouri, Indiana, Illinois, and Iowa. The regimental flag he died carrying was recovered by the British and sent back to London. It remains there on display as a war trophy. A Georgia county was also named for Sgt. John Newton, comrade to Jasper, in the incident freeing the American prisoners from the British at the spring near Savannah. Newton went on to fight in the Charleston siege but was captured and died of smallpox aboard a British prison ship.

Maj. Pierre-Charles L'Enfant led five-men through brisk musket fire on the day before the primary attack. His was a futile attempt to ignite the abatis in front of the British works. Critically wounded during the assault, he was left for dead on the field. It would be months before he could walk. L' Enfant would be appointed as the architect who laid out the plans for the city known for its magnificent scale and distances - Washington D.C.

John Laurens was one of the early advocates for

forming a black regiment to fight for liberty. It was not to be realized since most people felt the country was not ready. In 1780, he was sent as special minister to procure a loan from the French. Although he ran against protocol he was successful in his quest and returned home after six months. He rejoined Washington as a colonel at Yorktown and was allowed to negotiate the terms of surrender. Near the end of the war, he was appointed by Nathanael Greene to replace "Light Horse" Harry Lee when he retired as commander of his legion. In that capacity he arose from his sickbed to lead troops against a British expedition in search of provisions. The enemy lured him into an ambush and Laurens was hit. The wound proved fatal and Laurens was dead at age twenty-seven. It was felt that had he lived he would have served in George Washington's first cabinet.

Gen. Moultrie surrendered with the fall of Charleston in 1780. The capture of that city has been called the worst military defeat American history until Bataan in World War II. He was a prisoner on parole until 1782, when he was exchanged, and then again served the patriot cause until the end of the war. Afterwards, he was elected for two terms as South Carolina governor and served in the state senate between terms. He was also a member of the state convention that ratified the federal Constitution.

Gen. Samuel Elbert, after being captured at Briar Creek was finally released in 1781 on a prisoner exchange with the British. He immediately re-established himself in the army.   At Yorktown, he was in command of a brigade. After the war, he was elected as governor of Georgia. One of Savannah's squares is named in his honor as well as one of Georgia's counties.

Col. John Dooley was murdered by Tories in his home in Lincoln County in 1780 in the presence of his family.

Gen. John Ashe was so humiliated after his defeat at Briar Creek that he left the army and retired to private life in North Carolina. Gen. Ashe died of smallpox in 1781. The city of Asheville in North Carolina was named in his honor.

Col. Andrew Pickens was captured at the fall of Charleston and took an oath to sit out the war under British protection. However, when the British destroyed much of his property and terrorized his family, he again rebelled and recruited a militia to resume guerilla activities against the British. Pickens played a key role in the British defeat at the Battle of Cowpens. For his "spirited conduct" the Continental Congress presented him with a sword and the state of South Carolina promoted him to brigadier general in the state militia.

Col. George Walton, after his capture by the British in Savannah, was imprisoned until September 1779. The British knew the value of their prize and demanded a brigadier general in exchange. Finally he was released for a captain of the navy. In the following month, Walton was appointed governor of the state; and in the succeeding January, was elected a member of congress for two years. Walton was elected a representative to congress six different times; twice appointed governor of the state; once a senator of the United States; and at four different periods a judge of the superior court, which office he held for fifteen years, up until the time of his death.

Gen. Lachlan McIntosh retreated to Charleston with Lincoln and helped defend that city until the British took possession in May 1780. McIntosh was taken prisoner and not exchanged until February 1782. His confinement undermined his health. Eventually McIntosh returned to Georgia. In 1783 he was promoted to major general. He was elected to Congress in 1784. He was also appointed to help organize a treaty with the Indians that occupied the western part of Georgia. He died in 1806 in his native Savannah.

And what of the British? Gen. Prevost was accorded

from his officers a testimonial to his polite, disinterested and impartial behavior. He was credited with wisdom, vigilance and courage during the siege. Prevost died in 1786 waiting for a promotion that never materialized.

Col. Campbell was promoted to major general in 1782. He served as governor of Jamaica from 1781 to 1784 and governor of Madras from 1785 to 1789. He died in London in 1791.

Unfortunately, Col. John Maitland died October 25th, a few weeks after the siege. It was reported that after the attack, he retired to his quarters never to leave again. There was no question that he was ill the entire time of the action in Savannah. The man survived his day of glory but was unable to survive the villainous fever that had plagued him for weeks. Even in a weakened condition, he had remained in the trenches almost constantly since his arrival.

In Maitland's eulogy it stated his disposition was so amiable that to know him was to admire him. His manner was easy and engaging and his language strong and persuasive. His affability rendered him pleasing to every observer. Loved by his friends, respected by his acquaintances, and revered by every officer and soldier who had the good fortune to be in his command.

Maitland's services were overlooked when Gen. Prevost gave his official report to Lord George Germain, although he generously praised others. Others in Savannah, who had served with Maitland, only spoke with praise with no shred of anything derogatory to his character or personal habits. Most felt it was even providential that he lived as long as he did. The British officers in camp acknowledged with one voice the debt they owed for his bringing eight hundred men across an impassable marsh and swamp, all under the nose of enemy troops. Without them, Gen. Prevost's only option was surrender.

Even the American press in Charleston

acknowledged the allied defeat was due in large part to the presence and skill of an officer so indefatigable as Col. Maitland. The British historian, Charles Stedman wrote, "his memory will be dear to Britons so long as manly fortitude, unstained honor, and highly improved military talents, are held in estimation."

No other British soldier of the revolution received higher contemporary accolades than Maitland. His service inspired at least five poems. Unfortunately, his fame was soon forgotten. His was the state of most British heroes of the American Revolution, i.e., certainly not honored in America and forgotten at home as well. Maitland's remains were buried with all honors of war in the Colonial Cemetery in Savannah in the family vault of Lt. Gov. John Graham.

A few years later, the body of Gen. Nathanael Greene, commander of American Revolutionary forces in the South, was placed in the same vault. The tomb was opened the 1901 to transfer Greene's remains to a monument erected in his honor in Johnson Square in Savannah. Maitland's remains were not verified to be present and were not found until almost a century later in 1981. Then, they were transferred to his ancestral home in Haddington, Scotland.

Two years after the allied debacle at Savannah, a fresh opportunity for a Franco-American operation presented itself. Gen. George Washington's continentals, in cooperation with French regulars under Count Rochambeau and the French fleet under Admiral de Grasse, besieged Gen. Charles Cornwallis' British army at Yorktown. This time there were more favorable battle conditions, better coordination, and wiser command decisions.

On October 19, 1781, exactly two years after the rebel withdrawal from Savannah, Yorktown's eight thousand man British garrison surrendered. Gen. Lincoln's defeat in Savannah and later in Charleston in no way diminished Gen. Washington's respect for him. Lincoln was awarded the honor of receiving the sword of Lord Cornwallis during his surrender at Yorktown.

The defeat at Yorktown prompted Britain to open peace talks with the American rebels, and in early 1783 the Treaty of Paris recognized the United States as an independent nation.

It was all so long ago and yet seems almost like yesterday. The struggle for independence in Georgia has been largely forgotten by all but the most avid Revolutionary War historians. And yet it was here, in Georgia and in Savannah that such a pivotal point in the American Revolution was enacted.

Today, the battle and its hallowed ground are commemorated through a reconstruction of the Spring Hill redoubt and a historic marker noting what was the bloodiest hour of the Revolution. Hopefully, with increased awareness, all Americans will acknowledge their debt and gratitude for the price paid by their ancestors and allies in the struggle for independence in the South.

The End

Archibald Campbell

Robert Howe

Lachlan McIntosh

Button Gwinnett

Samuel Elbert

George Walton

Savannah Under Siege

Augustine Prevost

Benjamin Lincoln

Curt von Stedingk

Louis de Noailles

Arthur Dillon

John Maitland

Pulaski's Death Charge

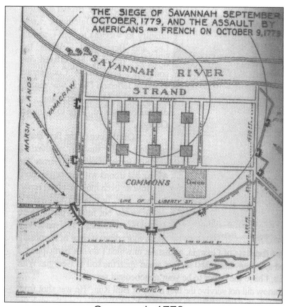

Savannah 1779

Savannah Under Siege

Siege of Savannah October 9, 1779

British Soldier   Grapeshot & Canister   French Soldier

H. Ronald Freeman

Charles C. Pinckney

Thomas Pinckney

Casimir Pulaski

John Rutledge

Admiral d'Estaing

John Laurens

References

Ashmore, Otis and Charles H. Olmstead, "A Story of the Revolution in Georgia, Being an Account of the Battle of Kettle Creek and the Battle of Briar Creek," Georgia Historical Quarterly, Savannah, Georgia, 1926.

The Siege of Savannah 1779, Advices from America as Published in the London Gazette, December 1779.

Boatner, Mark M. III, "Encyclopedia of the American Revolution," David MacKay Company, Inc., New York.

Campbell, Archibald, "The Journal of Lt. Colonel Archibald Campbell," The Ashantilly Press, Darien, Georgia, 1981.

Coulter, Merton, "History of Georgia," University of North Carolina Press, 1933.

Capps, Clifford S. and Eugenia Burney, "Colonial Georgia," Thomas Nelson Inc., Publishers, Nashville & New York, 1972.

Carrington, Henry B., "Battles of the American Revolution 1775-1781, Promontory Press, New York.

Chidsey, Donald Barr, "The War in the South," Crown Publishers, Inc., New York.

Coleman, Kenneth, "The American Revolution in Georgia, 1763 - 1789," University of Georgia Press, Athens, 1958.

Commager, Henry Steele and Richard B. Morris, "The Spirit of Seventy-Six," Harper & Row, Publishers, New York.

Coulter, Merton, University of North Carolina Press, 1933.

Crow, Jeffrey J and Larry E. Tise, "The Southern Experience in the American Revolution," The University of North Carolina Press, Chapel Hill.

Davis, Robert Scott, Jr., "Georgians in the Revolution: At Kettle Creek (Wilkes County) and Burke County, Southern Historical Press, Inc., Easly, S.C.

H. Ronald Freeman

Fleming, Thomas, "Liberty: The American Revolution," Viking, New York.

Flood, Charles Bracelen, "Rise, and Fight Again," Dodd, Mead, & Company, New York.

Thomas Gamble Collection, Chatham-Effingham Regional Library.

Harden, William, "A History of Savannah and South Georgia, Vol. I", Cherokee Publishing Co., Atlanta

The Georgia Historical Quarterly, Published by the Georgia Historical Society, Savannah.

Groover, Robert, "Sweet Land of Liberty," W.H. Wolfe Associates, Roswell, Georgia, 1987.

Hartley, Cecil B, "Heroes and Patriots of the South," G.G. Evans Publisher, Philadelphia, 1860.

Hibbert, Christopher, "Redcoats and Rebels: The American Revolution Through British Eyes, W.W. Norton & Company, New York.

Higgins, W. Robert, "The Revolutionary War in the South: Power, Conflict, and Leadership," John C. Cavanagh, American Military Leadership in the Southern Campaign: Benjamin Lincoln, Duke University Press, Durham, North Carolina.

Higgins, W. Robert, "The Revolutionary War in the South: Power, Conflict, and Leadership," Richard J. Hargrove, Portrait of a Southern Patriot: The Life and Death of John Laurens, Duke University Press, Durham, North Carolina.

Horry, Peter and M.L. Weems, "The Life of General Francis Marion," Joseph Allen, Philadelphia, 1854.

Hough, Franklin B., "The Siege of Savannah by the Combined American and French Forces, The Reprint Company Publishers, Spartanburg.

Howell, Clark, "History of Georgia," The S.J. Clarke Publishing Co., Chicago - Atlanta, 1926.

Jamro, R.D., "Pulaski: A Portrait of Freedom," Printcraft Press, Inc., Savannah, Georgia,

Savannah Under Siege

Jones, Charles, C. Jr., "History of Savannah, Georgia," D. Mason & Co., Syracuse, New York, 1890.

Jones, Charles C. Jr., "The Siege of Savannah by the Fleet of Count d'Estaing in 1779," The New York Times and Arno Press, Albany, N.Y.

Kennedy, Benjamin, "Muskets, Cannon Balls & Bombs: Nine Narratives of the Siege of Savannah in 1779, The Beehive Press, Savannah.

Killion, Ronald G. and Charles T. Waller, "Georgia and the Revolution," Cherokee Publishing Company, Atlanta, 1975.

Knight, Lucian Lamar, "A Standard History of Georgia and Georgians," The Lewis Publishing Co., Chicago - New York, 1917.

Lawrence, Alexander A., "Storm Over Savannah," The University of Georgia Press, Athens, 1951.

Lee, Henry, "The American Revolution in the South," Arno Press, New York.

Lumpkin, Henry B., "From Savannah to Yorktown."

McCall, Capt. Hugh, "The History of Georgia," Reprinted by A.B. Caldwell, Atlanta.

Morrill, Dan L., "Southern Campaigns of the American Revolution," The Nautical and Aviation Publishing Company of America, Mt. Pleasant, South Carolina.

Moultrie, William, "Memoirs of the American Revolution: So far as it related to the states of North and South Carolina and Georgia," Printed by David Longworth, New York, 1802.

Pancake, John S., "This Destructive War: The British Campaign in the Carolinas, 1780-1782, The University of Alabama Press, 1985.

Pinkowski, Edward, "General Pulaski's Body," Presented in October 1997 at the Pulaski Museum in Warka, Poland

Russell, Preston and Barbara Hines, "Savannah: A

History of Her People Since 1733," Frederic C. Beil, Publisher, Savannah, Ga., 1992.

Scheer, George F. and Hugh F. Rankin, "Rebels and Redcoats," The World Publishing Company, Cleveland and New York.

Scruggs, Carroll Proctor, "Georgia During the Revolution," Bay Tree Grove, Publishers, Norcross, Ga., 1976.

Shaw, Terry, "Bonaventure Historical Society Newsletter," October 1996, Savannah, Georgia.

Smith, Page, "A New Age Now Begins," McGraw-Hill Book Company, New York.

Standard, Janet Harvill, "The Battle of Kettle Creek," Wilkes Publishing Co, Inc., Washington, Georgia

Stedman, Charles, "The Origin, Progress, and Termination of the American War," Published by the Author, London, 1794.

Stevens, William Bacon, "A History of Georgia," Beehive Press, Savannah 1972.

Stember, Sol, "The Bicentennial Guide to the American Revolution: Volume III, The War in the South," Saturday Review Press/E.P. Dutton & Co., Inc., New York.

Weeks, Carl Solana, "Savannah: In the Time of Peter Tondee, The Road to Revolution in Colonial Georgia," Summerhouse Press, Columbia, S.C., 1997.

Wheeler, Richard, "Voices of 1776," Thomas Y. Crowell Company, New York.

Wilson, Adelaide Wilson, "Historic and Picturesque Savannah," The Boston Photogravure Company, 1889.

Illustration Credits

Battle of Savannah - Ga. Dept. of Archives and History
British & French Soldier - John H. Batchelor - Armies of the
American Revolution, Prentice-Hall Inc.
D'Estaing, Charles-Henri - V. and J. Duncan Antique Maps
and Prints
De Noailles, Louis - V. and J. Duncan Antique Maps and
Prints
Dillon, Arthur - Lawrence, Alexander, "Storm Over
Savannah"
Elbert, Samuel - Georgia Historical Society
Gwinnett, Button - University of Georgia Library.
Laurens, John - U.S. Army Center of Military History
Lincoln, Benjamin - Independence National Historical Park,
Philadelphia
Maitland, John - Georgia Historical Society
McIntosh, Lachlan - CEL Library, Gamble Collection.
Pinckney, Charles Cotesworth - The Nat'l Portrait Gallery
Pinckney, Thomas - The South Carolina Library
Prevost, Augustine - Margaret Prevost Wood
Pulaski, Casimir - Ga. Department of Archives and History
Pulaski's Death - Stanislaw Batowski, "The Death of
General Casimir Pulaski," 1933. The Polish
Museum of America
Rutledge, John - V. and J. Duncan Antique Maps and
Prints
Savannah Siege Map - University of Georgia Library,
Hargrett Collection
Von Stedingk, Curt - J.N. Le Monnier 1802.
Walton, George - University of Georgia Library

H. Ronald Freeman

Index

Bryan, Jonathan· 26
Bulloch, Archibald· 2
Bunker Hill· 85, 135
Butler, Pierce· 66, 152

A

Abatis· 76
Allen, Ethan· 9
Amelia Island· 12
Anderson, Capt.· 35
Annibal· 58
Antoinette, Marie· 61, 62, 147, 148
Ariel· 92
Ashe, John· 40, 41, 42, 43, 44, 45, 153
Augusta· 1, 4, 29, 34, 35, 36, 39, 40, 46, 48, 65, 67, 68, 84, 157
Augusta Road· 23, 24, 72, 77, 105, 109, 118, 119, 121, 123, 130, 132

B

Baird, James· 19, 23, 42, 44
Baker, John· 12, 13, 16, 68
Beaufort· 32, 40, 52, 55, 57, 58, 70, 75, 80, 82, 94
Beaulieu· 4, 59, 71, 72, 84, 88
Bentalou, Capt.· 125, 127
Betisy, Col.· 110, 120, 123
Black Swamp· 46
Bonaventure· 72, 166
Bougainville, Louis-Antoine· 59, 141
Boyd, James· 34, 35, 36, 37, 38, 39, 40
Brewton Hill· 20, 21, 81
Briar Creek· 40, 41, 43, 44, 45, 46, 68, 75, 153, 163
Brown, Thomas· 105, 110, 119

C

Callibogue Sound· 79
Campbell, Archibald· 8, 9, 10, 15, 19, 21, 22, 23, 26, 27, 29, 32, 34, 36, 39, 40, 45, 75, 114, 155, 163
Cesar· 58
Champion· 92
Charleston· 6, 29, 30, 31, 33, 46, 48, 49, 54, 55, 63, 65, 67, 82, 93, 94, 99, 101, 107, 111, 128, 129, 136, 137, 141, 145, 152, 153, 154, 155, 156
Cherokee Hill· 26, 57, 67, 72
Christophe, Henri· 62
Clarke, Elijah· 35, 37
Clinton, Henry· 8, 10, 25, 34, 82, 107, 144
Comet· 20, 80, 122
Cruger, John· 57, 83, 106, 117

D

Dallemangne, Claude· 63
Daufuskie Island· 79
Dauphin Royal· 58
Diademe· 58
Dillon, Arthur· 62, 73, 86, 106, 110, 113, 114, 115, 117,

119, 120, 123, 139, 141,
142, 148
Dolly, Quamino· 22
Dooley, John· 34, 35, 37, 38,
153

E

East Florida· 10, 12
Ebenezer· 14, 29, 30, 57, 65,
109
Elbert, Samuel· 11, 12, 13, 14,
17, 20, 22, 24, 42, 43, 68,
153
Elliott, Mrs. Barnard· 129
Experiment· 92, 93

F

Fair Lawn· 22, 76, 115
Fantasque· 58
Fendant· 58
Few, William· 98, 152
Fier Rodrigue· 58
Fort Sullivan· 29
Frederica· 12, 13
French, Capt.· 70, 71, 94, 95,
126, 137, 139, 142, 153
Fort Morris· 15, 17
Fort Wayne· 22, 106
Fuser, Lewis· 15, 17, 18

G

Garth, George· 93
Germain· 106, 112, 122, 155
Germain, Lord George· 155
Glascock, Thomas· 128
Graham, John· 92, 93, 98, 156
Grapeshot· 121
Gray, James· 129

Greene, Nathanael· 66, 86,
153, 156
Greenwich· 20, 137, 139
Guerrier· 58
Gwinnett, Button· 2, 10, 11,
12, 14, 65, 87

H

Habersham, Joseph· 2, 68, 71,
72, 152
Hamilton, Paul· 57, 117
Hector· 58
Hessians· 8, 50, 51, 70
Heyward, Thomas· 66
Highlanders· 8, 20, 21, 24, 42,
44, 51, 57, 70, 113, 118
Horry, Peter· 66, 125, 127,
128, 164
Houstoun, John· 26, 27, 68
Howe, Robert· 10, 15, 19, 20,
21, 22, 23, 26, 27, 31, 32
Huger, Isaac· 22, 24, 66, 116,
117
Hume, Alexander· 129
Hutchinson Island· 78, 96, 99

I

Innes, Col.· 25

J

Jackson, James· 68, 152
Jasper, William· 29, 30, 33, 66,
129, 130, 152, 167
Jefferson, Thomas· 143, 152
Johns Island· 50, 51
Jones, John· 98, 100, 137
Jones, John Paul· 58, 60
Jourdan, Jean-Baptiste· 63

H. Ronald Freeman

K

Keppel· 20, 80
Kettle Creek· 34, 36, 39, 40, 45, 163, 166
King George· 3, 8, 57, 144
King Louis XVI· 3

L

Lafayette, Marquis de· 3, 62, 96, 139, 140, 144
Languedoc· 58, 59, 96, 147 135, 152, 164
Laurens, Henry· 14, 66
Laurens, John· 66, 110, 111, 128, 129, 135, 152
Lee, Henry· 165
Lincoln, Benjamin· 6, 7, 19, 20, 26, 27, 31, 32, 40, 41, 44, 45, 46, 48, 49, 50, 51, 52, 53, 54, 55, 57, 63, 65, 67, 68, 70, 72, 81, 82, 84, 85, 86, 87, 88, 93, 94, 95, 108, 110, 113, 114, 125, 136, 138, 139, 141, 142, 153, 154, 156

M

Magnifique· 58, 103
Maitland, John· 20, 21, 50, 51, 52, 55, 57, 70, 74, 75, 79, 80, 81, 82, 83, 84, 94, 95, 98, 110, 112, 115, 118, 123, 124, 128, 130, 133, 140, 155, 156
Marion, Francis· 66, 84
McGirth, Daniel· 12, 13, 16, 35, 39, 40
McIntosh , John· 17, 42, 43

McIntosh, Lachlan· 11, 65, 68, 98, 154
Midway· 4, 16, 17
Minis, Philip· 71
Moultrie, William· 32, 33, 40, 41, 45, 46, 48, 49, 50, 51, 67, 153, 165
Musgrove Creek· 24, 105, 106
Myrtle· 92

N

Napoleon Bonaparte· 58, 63, 115
Newton, John· 29, 30, 152
Noailles, Louis-Marie de· 61, 86, 96, 106, 107, 110, 118, 133, 139, 141, 148, 149

O

Ogeechee· 4, 17, 57, 58, 65, 72, 82, 86, 87
Oglethorpe· 4, 136
Orangeburg· 46, 48, 49

P

Phoenix· 46
Pinckney, Charles Cotesworth· 67, 152
Pinckney, Thomas· 67, 93, 130, 152
Pollard, Ensign· 97
Port Royal· 52, 82
Prevost, Augustine· 6, 10, 11, 15, 16, 17, 18, 19, 20, 28, 29, 32, 40, 41, 42, 45, 46, 48, 49, 50, 51, 52, 56, 57, 70, 71, 73, 74, 75, 79, 81, 82, 84, 85, 93, 94, 97, 98,

99, 100, 105, 111, 112, 135, 144, 154, 155, 167
Prevost, Marc· 15, 41
Provence· 58
Pulaski, Casimir· 65, 68, 69, 72, 86, 109, 111, 125, 126, 127, 128, 129, 136, 137
Purysburg· 26, 29, 31, 32, 40, 48, 65, 67

R

Robuste· 58
Rose· 78
Rutledge, John· 30, 46, 48, 49, 54, 63, 67, 130, 141

S

Sagittaire· 58, 92
Scarborough· 2
Sheldon· 52, 53, 57
Silk Hope· 72
Spring Hill· 77, 104, 105, 106, 109, 110, 112, 116, 119, 121, 124, 125, 126, 128, 138, 141, 142
Springfield Plantation· 86, 136
St. Augustine· 10, 11, 12, 13, 15, 17, 75
Stokes, Anthony· 97
Stono Ferry· 48, 50, 57, 65, 70
Sunbury· 1, 12, 14, 15, 16, 17, 18, 19, 28, 42, 57, 82, 83, 98, 106

T

Tattnall plantation· 22, 115
Tattnall, Josiah· 22, 76, 115
Tawes, Thomas· 112

Thunder· 122
Thunderbolt· 4, 72, 88, 139, 141
Tomochichi· 4
Tonnant· 58
Treutlen, John· 14
Truite· 96
Trustees' Garden· 4
Tybee· 19, 56, 57, 58, 70, 77, 79, 90, 98, 137

V

Vaillant· 58
Vengeur· 58
Victory· 92
Vigilante· 20, 79
Von Stedingk, Curt· 62, 95, 106, 110, 111, 113, 114, 118, 123, 124, 128, 132, 148, 149

W

Wallace, James· 92
Walton, George· 14, 22, 23, 154
Washington, George· 3, 6, 10, 14, 21, 31, 38, 66, 96, 140, 143, 152, 153, 156, 157
Wasp· 137
White, John· 23, 58, 68
Wright, James· 2, 27, 56, 74, 76, 92, 98, 106, 117, 137, 144

Y

Yamacraw· 4, 77, 111, 122, 125

Z

Zele· 58

Zubley's Ferry· 4, 26, 67, 84